CHARL⏻TTE VIEWPOINT

PERSPECTIVES

CHARLOTTE VIEWPOINT

PERSPECTIVES

Mark Peres
Editorial Direction

Russell Shuler
Art Direction

Paul Cotter
Mark Peres
Russell Shuler
Photography

Mark Peres
Poetry

Published by John F. Blair, Publisher
Winston-Salem, North Carolina

The paper in this book meets the guidelines for permanence and durability of the Committee on Production Guidelines for Book Longevity of the Council on Library Resources.

This project was made possible, in part,
through grants and contributions from:

Arts & Science Council
Charlotte Regional Visitors Authority
Goodrich Corporation
Leadership Charlotte
Luquire George Andrews

Design by Russell Shuler
Cover Photo by Paul Cotter

This book is printed on acid-free paper.
Printed in Korea

Library of Congress Cataloging-in-Publication Data

Charlotte viewpoint : perspectives / edited by Mark Peres.
        p.   cm.
ISBN-13: 978-0-89587-338-5 (alk. paper)
ISBN-10: 0-89587-338-9 (alk. paper)
  1. City planning—North Carolina—Charlotte.
  2. Land use—North Carolina—Charlotte.
    3. Charlotte (N.C.) I. Peres, Mark.

HT168.C456C436 2006
307.1'21675676--dc22
2006027477

Contents

CONTENTS (CONTINUED)

INTRODUCTION

In November 2003, we published the inaugural issue of *Charlotte ViewPoint* magazine on our website: www.charlotteviewpoint.org. The monthly online magazine explores the dynamics of Charlotte, and has evolved to offer what we think is the best commentary and photography in the city. The magazine does not have advertisers. All who contribute to it do so as volunteers.

As far we knew, it was the first non-commercial, web-based, art and opinion magazine that spoke to a city's urban life and future. It was decidedly an amateur effort, and it is still today. We launched the magazine to offer citizens a platform to speak in their own voice, and to help guide the body politic toward a point of view that celebrates the best of city living.

As we've noted elsewhere, the magazine has allowed us to visit with friends – a decidedly Charlottean pursuit. Relationships matter. They enrich our view of the world, they strengthen what we can achieve collectively, and they offer shared experiences that give us memories and fulfillment. Charlotte is a city that is growing in leaps and bounds, yet functions one friendship at a time.

In the fall of 2006, Charlotte ViewPoint became a non-profit literary and educational organization. Our mission is thought leadership about city life and urban issues. We aim in our publications and public forums to offer an experience not unlike a good, spirited conversation at a café, where, oh by the way, one of us brings his or her photo album to share. We hope to advance civic culture with thoughtful exchange, while capturing the rhythms and seasons of urban living. We invite your support of our mission.

This book is the result of an idea first raised by Paul Cotter, a remarkable photographer and good friend. Many others played an indispensable role in the idea's journey to reality, including Patricia Zoder, Smokey Oats, Kelly Chopus and Jennifer Garner who helped us meet challenges and keep our momentum going. Carolie Bartol, a founding member of our team, lent great insights in refining the art direction for this book. However, if there is one person who deserves our lasting gratitude for this project, it is Russell Shuler. Russell has given exceptional time and extraordinary talent to this effort.

We also wish to thank the sponsors of this book who made this project possible: Arts & Science Council, Charlotte Regional Visitors Authority, Goodrich Corporation, Leadership Charlotte and Luquire George Andrews. We also wish to thank our partners Carolyn Sakowski and Angela Harwood at John F. Blair, Publisher.

Lastly, all of us at Charlotte ViewPoint magazine thank our contributors and readers. Charlotte is blessed with many of the finest leaders in the nation, many of whom have graced our pages. Our sincerest thanks to our readers who represent the most highly-informed and engaged citizens in the region.

Mark Peres

I first saw Charlotte in the summer of 1998, when my family was checking out several cities to decide where we wanted to live. We stayed at an uptown hotel, assuming that's where we'd feel the real pulse of the region. Unfortunately, the Center City's heartbeat at that time was just a barely perceptible murmur. As we walked, we saw lots of chrome and glass, and plenty of parking lots. I kept wondering where the city's soul was hiding. Where were the coffee shops? The wine bars? The delis? We asked someone where we might grab breakfast on a Saturday morning. "Hmmm, that's a good question," he said, scratching his head. Then he directed us out to the suburbs somewhere.

That was 1998. Since then, the paddles have been placed on the Center City's chest, a powerful jolt's been applied, and the heart is thumping vigorously. I'm glad to say that my wife, kids and I sensed it coming. We built a house in the revitalized First Ward, and we've watched our Uptown neighborhood and the whole center city come to life. When you walk down Tryon Street on a weeknight now, you see more than clean sidewalks. You see crowds of people – young singles hitting the bars, couples sipping wine outside cozy bistros, parents having dinner with their kids, fans pouring out from the new Uptown arena.

As a photographer, I love shooting for Charlotte ViewPoint because it encourages me to keep my eyes open. I try to look at the city through the fresh eyes of a newcomer, even though I've lived here for several years now. Take a look around. You'll see beautiful details everywhere. And plenty of hidden surprises.

Paul Cotter

Having lived in Charlotte since 1990, I've seen the city go through many, many changes. Friends have come and gone. The city has grown in all directions. Through it all, one thing has remained the same: Charlotte's focus on the future.

My contribution to Charlotte ViewPoint is to offer skills in photography and design. Being an art director all my life, I have seen the power of well-placed, well-timed messages. It is my sincere hope that this collection of Perspectives will cause Charlotte to take an even more sober and long-term view in its decision-making processes. My more immediate hope, however, is that you enjoy this collection right now.

Russell Shuler

Q&A WITH JIM PALERMO
BY MARK PERES

MARCH 2005

Jim Palermo is a resident of Fourth Ward and former chairman of Charlotte Center City Partners. Jim retired as an executive vice president for Bank of America. Jim has served as chairman of the Charlotte Arts & Science Council, as president of the Friends of Fourth Ward, and served as a director of the North Carolina Medical Foundation. Currently, Jim serves as chair of the Charlotte Chamber of Commerce Economic Development Committee, is president of the Charlotte-Mecklenburg Police Foundation and is Co-chair of the Brain Tumor Fund for the Carolinas.

You have been active for many years in helping develop the Center City. Why is a vibrant Center City important?

Cities need a center as a wheel must have a hub. We know the spokes are joined together by the hub. Roads, rail lines, and bike paths need a place to start and end. Cities without a solid core become dysfunctional: Transportation grids and well-thought out land plans become difficult, and uncontrolled sprawl pulls hard on the vibrancy of the central region. Charlotte has a core. Well-thought-out road grids, and soon rail lines, will feed that core. Continued investment from both the private sector and public arena will cause tax revenue from the Center City to increase. At the same time, the infrastructure investment stays constant. Most often overlooked is that the Charlotte core is an "exporter" of tax revenue. Government data suggests that four out of every five tax dollars produced in the Center City are used outside the core. In other words, it makes good business sense to protect that vibrancy as it is currently supporting most of what is going on in the rest of the city.

Where is the Center City now within Charlotte's historical context?

The Center City is riding a crest. However, we all know that it has not always been the case. Going back in history, we have seen the center of Charlotte go up and down several times. The advent of the trolley and the subsequent growth of suburban shopping altered the core's stability. But at this point in time, we are absolutely in the right place.

What are the most critical elements of the Center City that you believe citizens must support?

Three areas as I see it: First, we must keep our neighborhoods safe. Today we are the safest precinct in the city. However, police understaffing can threaten that record. Second, we need to push government to be sensitive to the changing environment. Transportation experts who want to only move cars from point A to point B will likely run over our kids in the process. They didn't have to worry about pedestrians when the Center City was empty, but it's different now. Third, let's not make foolish economic moves. What has worked should be protected. Taking success for granted will bring on the reoccurrence of a down cycle that will hurt everyone.

What current threats do you see to the continued growth of the Center City?

The idea of taxing downtown parking or doubling the municipal services tax (which is a property tax paid by Uptown residents as well as businesses) will rip the economic insides out of the Center City. I support additional cultural venues in our community, but I disagree that they should be paid for by one neighborhood when they benefit everyone. Also, the process of coming up with what should be included in the arts package and how it should be paid for was flawed. Today, the package contains a wish list. It seems like everyone just piled on. We need to make sure that groups studying the arts and taxes are representative. Leaders and citizens of the Center City need to be part of those discussions.

What interests you most about the future of Charlotte?

The future looks bright. Every week another high-rise condo project is announced and it is soon sold out. The arrival of Johnson & Wales and the thought of 4,000 students feeding our economy is exciting. Center City Charlotte is positioned to become one of the most desirable neighborhoods in the city. That future will be strengthened by good leadership. With Hugh McColl retired, others will need to help fill the void. While we are treading water with leadership today, a little shot in the arm will get us swimming again. ⏻

Q&A with John Lassiter

By Mark Peres

February 2005

John Lassiter is an at-large member of the Charlotte City Council. John serves as chair of the Economic Development/Planning Council Committee and is a member of the Restructuring Government and Governmental Affairs Council Committees. John formerly served on the Charlotte-Mecklenburg Board of Education, and has been on the board of directors of Junior Achievement, Dowd YMCA and Children's Law Center. He received his BA degree from Wake Forest University in 1976, an MPA from North Carolina State University in 1977 and his law degree from Wake Forest University in 1980. John is president and CEO of Carolina Legal Staffing.

You serve as Chair of the City's Economic Development Planning Committee. What development projects are you currently reviewing?

Our committee has been reviewing several projects, including the development plans for a new Wachovia tower across from the Convention Center that will include a 1,200-seat theatre that may house the North Carolina Dance Theatre as well as the Charlotte campus of the Wake Forest University School of Business. This project is the first of several projects recommended in the Arts & Science Council's Long-Range Cultural Facilities Plan. We are also working on development alternatives for city-owned parcels of land adjacent to the new Arena. In the past several months, we have completed our review of the revitalization project for Midtown Square, the Epicenter project on the old convention center property and the Elizabeth Avenue redevelopment project. All three of these efforts will convert underdeveloped and abandoned land uses to Center City retail, restaurants and entertainment venues.

How do you determine what private projects deserve public monies or tax subsidies?

In the past, private projects have requested public funding on an ad-hoc basis, often resulting in a lack of scrutiny and questionable support by many taxpayers. We have developed an evaluation tool called the "Sustainability Index" that measures how a particular project may meet a variety of community goals – revitalizing a corridor or creating housing alternatives – as well as evaluating the financial plan for the project. Before a project will be considered for public investment, it must have a high score on the Sustainability Index and be unable to develop "but for" some public investment. Our investments can include transportation, sidewalk or streetscape improvements or possibly the use of future taxes on the improved property to fund parking decks needed to support the retail, housing or commercial office uses in the project.

You serve on the Mayor's Task Force on the Arts. What core recommendation is the Task Force making about the future of the arts in the City?

The Task Force met for several months this past summer and fall to consider the recommendations made in the ASC's Long-Range Cultural Facilities Plan. The group, composed of both representatives of the affiliated arts organizations and members of City Council, unanimously agreed on several far-reaching proposals. First, all of the projects deserve consideration for renovation, relocation or construction. These projects include a complete renovation of Discovery Place and the Afro-American Cultural Center, the relocation of the Mint Museum to a Center City location, the construction of a 1,200-seat theatre for the North Carolina Dance Theatre and a home for the Bechtler modern art collection. Second, the city should focus its efforts and funding on facility construction and maintenance rather than operations. Because the city can leverage its investment through bonds on 12:1 ratio, operating subsidies should be transferred to capital construction and let the users and patrons of the cultural facilities focus on operating and program expenses. Third, co-location, joint use and consolidation of "back of house" expenses like ticketing, security and custodial can result in significant cost savings, and allow the arts affiliates to focus on programming. City Council will devote time at its annual retreat in February to consider the complete recommendations of the Task Force.

You also serve on the working committee to bring the NASCAR Hall of Fame to Charlotte. What is underway for us to win the selection?

NASCAR has asked four cities – Charlotte, Atlanta, Daytona and Kansas City – to respond to a Request for Proposal to build a Hall of Fame museum. Responses will be due in May of 2005. The mayor has appointed a working committee including Cathy Bessant of Bank of America and current Chair of the Charlotte Chamber, Luther Cochrane, Chair of the Charlotte Regional Visitors Authority, and Tim Newman, recently named President of the CVRA and formerly President of Center City Partners. The group will begin meeting in early February to develop a plan of action for Charlotte's proposal. Clearly, this opportunity is a way to cement NASCAR's connection to our community and link Lowe's Motor Speedway, dozens of race teams based in the area and the automotive engineering programs at UNC Charlotte. Charlotte recognizes the importance racing has for our regional economy and the health of our hospitality and tourism industry.

What is your vision of Charlotte in five years?

Charlotte has been and will continue to be the economic engine for the region and take on an increasing greater role in the economic health of both North and South Carolina. New businesses large and small will choose Charlotte for relocation and expansion. The Center City will not only continue to produce new jobs but provide housing to several thousand more residents, provide a wider variety of entertainment options, including more cultural options, more professional sports including both basketball and baseball, and, for the first time in decades, have significant retail activity. All of these efforts will be tied to a transportation system that allows residents from booming suburban communities to travel to and through the Center City by train, bus and automobile. Pedestrian-friendly streetscapes and greenways will link residential, educational and commercial uses throughout the city. New educational institutions, like Johnson & Wales and Queens University Law School will combine with Johnson C. Smith University, UNC Charlotte and CPCC to train the creative and skilled workers our community will need to compete in the global economy. ⏻

THE INTELLECTUAL LIFE OF A CITY

BY DR. PAMELA DAVIES, PRESIDENT, QUEENS UNIVERSITY OF CHARLOTTE

MAY 2006

*W*isdom *begins in wonder* ~ Socrates

At the heart of great cities are great universities. As we look at Charlotte and the many and varied institutions of higher education in our city, Charlotte is indeed a great city. We are blessed with a variety of educational institutions, each offering a unique and valuable educational path. With cutting-edge research and technology at UNC Charlotte, culinary and hospitality degrees at Johnson & Wales, technical and training fields at Central Piedmont Community College, and the long-standing liberal arts traditions at Davidson College, Johnson C. Smith and Queens University of Charlotte, there is every kind of education available in and around Charlotte. Although Charlotte is not yet seen as a "college town" like Boston or Chicago, we do have opportunities as citizens of Charlotte to experience the academic life offered by these colleges and universities. All of these Charlotte institutions offer programs, speakers and events that explore a variety of cultural, political and social issues.

Queens has long believed that a city college should not be an ivory tower on a hill, removed from the hustle and bustle of real life. A university should be part of the city, and open its doors to all citizens, not just those students fortunate enough to walk the halls and attend classes. I recently heard Charlotte Business Woman of the Year Winner Christie Taylor encourage us to be more curious in life. We can certainly engage our curiosity with the wealth of cultural, athletic and academic programs offered by the colleges and universities in town.

We can go to lunch at Johnson & Wales and enjoy the delicious fruits of the labor of the next generation of chefs. We can enjoy an opera in the new Dale F. Halton Theater at CPCC. We can hear activists like Judy Shephard at Davidson College and we can cheer on Division I athletes at UNC Charlotte.

11

Charlotte Magazine just named the Learning Society at Queens University of Charlotte a "Best of the Best" Award Recipient for Best Lecture Series. The Learning Society is a group of leading Charlotteans whose membership fees provide the major funding for a national speaker series, providing Queens students and the Charlotte community with the opportunity to interact with experts on important contemporary issues and topics. This year the Learning Society hosted author John Irving, journalist Charles Krauthammer, and will bring David McCullough and Bill Moyers to Charlotte next year. Learning Society members take very seriously their mission to bring acclaimed speakers to Charlotte for a learning experience that might otherwise not be possible for our students and citizens.

As part of Queens University's Sesquicentennial celebration of 150 years in Charlotte, a variety of activities and events are planned for the intellectual life at Queens and the city. The Friends of Library hosts Joyce Carol Oates; The Friends of Music will bring The Julliard String Quartet and the Chatham County Line blue grass group to our city. The Friends of Art sponsored feminist artist Judy Chicago this spring at Queens. The Norris and Kathryn Preyer Lecture series brings a speaker on the liberal arts to campus, and the William and Margaret Witherspoon Lecture series focuses on the intersection between science and religion.

I encourage everyone to be a citizen of a great city and continue to learn, be curious and engage your intellect. While we may have left behind the classrooms of our childhood, we are never too old to keep learning and to participate in the life of the mind. The intellectual life of a city is an important part of our growth as a world-class community. As citizens, we must engage in public debate and discuss together as a community those issues that face us and our nation together. At the heart of the liberal arts is the ability to reason and debate. We owe it to ourselves and the favorite teachers of our past to keep learning. We can build the intellectual capital of Charlotte by the lively engagement of our minds.

"Education is not the filling of a pail, but the lighting of a fire." – William Butler Yeats ⏻

Dreams of ice

Windswept air

Canticles of blue

CHARLOTTE'S CULTURAL SYSTEM:
FROM THE COMMUNITY, TO THE COMMUNITY

BY LEE KEESLER, PRESIDENT & CEO, ARTS AND SCIENCE COUNCIL

NOVEMBER 2004

Consider, for a moment, the details of a time-tested Charlotte business that still brims with opportunity. Here are just a few of its selling points:

· Customers use its products close to 3 million times in a fiscal year

· Investors number 40,000 annually

· It generates $100 million in economic impact, putting the potential price tag for this business at a half billion dollars or more

· Over 2,000 jobs created

· More than 8,000 dedicated volunteers ensure its success

I am referring to the cultural system that we enjoy in Charlotte-Mecklenburg.

What is the cultural system? The cultural system that exists in our city is a gift from the community, to the community. Cultural organizations, individual and corporate donors, businesses, government, artists, educators and patrons all play important roles in this vibrant and essential enterprise. Arts, science and history organizations provide considerable benefits to our region. It is difficult to find anyone whose life isn't enhanced by them both personally and economically. From young people touring a science exhibit or hearing their first orchestra concert to thousands who visit museums or attend opening nights at the theatre, these organizations host more than 55,000 events annually that educate, enlighten, enrich and entertain. Beyond the obvious, our cultural organizations provide untold contributions to the quality of life in Charlotte-Mecklenburg. The cultural system increases capital on many fronts. It brings workplace capital to the region as an attractor of new companies. It is an incubator for new social capital, encouraging citizens to become involved in important community issues. It helps us retain intellectual capital and transforms it into creative capital, one of the many keys to a thriving community.

Why should we pay attention to our cultural system? Charlotte has enjoyed incredible growth over the last 25 years, and investment in the cultural system has played a pivotal role. Culture has helped our city move forward. The Cultural Action Plan of 1976 detailed recommendations for a science museum, studio space for artists and an Afro-American Cultural and Service Center, just to name a few. Today, when we look at Charlotte's Center City, institutions such as Discovery Place, the McColl Center for Visual Art and the Afro-American Cultural Center are monuments of forward thinking and careful planning. In 1958, when the Arts & Science Council (ASC) was formed, the $63,000 it raised supported eight anchor cultural organizations. Today, the ASC will reinvest more than $13 million back into the system to help support 27 cultural organizations, individual artists and community organizations that provide neighborhood cultural programs.

How will the cultural system navigate the next 25 years? Clearly, our unique cultural system makes Charlotte a better place to live, work, play, visit, move to and raise a family. A new cultural facilities plan for the next 25 years has been completed and presents ideas ranging from a renovated Discovery Place to a new 1,200-seat theater and the creation of a new museum housing a collection of modern art courtesy of the philanthropic spirit of Andreas Bechtler. Business leaders, cultural leaders and elected officials are engaged in dialogue that could mean a dynamic new face for our cultural institutions and a renewed focus on the importance of cultural infrastructure. The time is now to champion the increasing needs of our art, science and history groups so they remain state-of-the-art and poised to meet the demands of our growing community for years to come. Historically, support of culture has proven to be a sound investment with high returns. At ASC, we continue to advance the system in hopes of leaving it better for the generations that follow us. We respectfully thank all those who contribute to this cultural enterprise and make it work for the greater good with gifts from the community, to the community. ⏻

Q&A with Sally Van Allen
By Mark Peres

June 2004

Sally Van Allen serves on the Board of Directors of the Carolina Theater Preservation Society. Sally has been active in the arts in Charlotte since 1950, serving in several leadership roles, including as president of the Charlotte Junior League.

Tell us about the Carolina Theater.

The Carolina is a magnificent historic theater built in 1927 that was once the center of Charlotte's art and culture and could very will be again. In mid-century, there were several theaters downtown, including the Broadway, Imperial, Charlotte and Alhambra. The Carolina was the grandest of them all, and is now the only one left standing. The motif was atmospheric. When you were inside, you felt you were in outdoor gardens. I remember watching the Broadway production of *Mr. Roberts*, and later the openings of *Dr. Zhivago* and *The Sound of Music*. It was and is a special place.

Why is it important that we renovate it?

We've saved so little of our history. If Charlotte doesn't have a soul, it's because it chooses not to have one. This is an opportunity to reclaim our traditions. Our past is as important as our future in defining our identity. I was pleased to see MecDec Day revived. Renovating the Carolina is a similar opportunity. The historic theaters from the Roaring 20s are unique. Grand historic theaters that have been reclaimed draw thousands of visitors because of their amazing beauty. The structure of the Carolina is in great shape and prime for renovation.

Is a renovated Carolina Theater compatible with the proposed Bechtler Museum?

Yes, but the current plans for the Bechtler call for the near total destruction of the Carolina as a working space. If we pause and reconsider the architecture, the Bechtler can build beside, up and over in a cantilever design. The two in combination would be spectacular. Just imagine a modern contemporary museum of art combined with a stunning renovation of a grand historic theater. That corner would own the city. Programming would not compete with opera, dance or large productions. Instead, the Carolina would serve more intimate music, comedy and plays, including tours that currently bypass the city. It would be a perfect historic place for town hall meetings and civic debate. Each citizen worth his or her salt needs to spend a long afternoon inside the Carolina, imagining the possibilities, deciding what's right and getting the courage to do something about it. ⏻

One Charlotte

By Patrick Mumford, Charlotte City Counciil Member, At-Large

December 2005

What defines a city, causing it to stand out amongst its peers, to be a place of attraction? Is it a strong school system, good roads, a vibrant downtown, overall affordability, safe neighborhoods or plentiful job opportunities? Or is it an overall quality of life that emanates from a broad park system, a clean environment or various arts and entertainment options? It is not any single attribute, but rather all of these, urban and suburban, that make a city desirable. Charlotte's future viability is dependent on the successful and responsible balancing of these seemingly disparate areas of interest.

Advances in technology, cultural shifts and changing social norms are causing people to reconsider what they value. Young, single professionals are seeking to live in places that emphasize transportation choices, lifestyle options, and interactive amenities. Parents want a system of high-quality education, well-maintained parks and good roads. Corporations, in an effort to attract and retain the best employees, desire cultural venues for the arts and entertainment. The working poor yearn for affordable housing options in safe neighborhoods. New arrivals from other countries hope to find an acceptance of cultural differences and opportunities that embrace diversity. Seniors, especially those on a fixed income, are concerned with overall affordability.

The manner in which each of these issues is addressed is of personal importance to those directly affected. Some are solely focused on downtown initiatives, while others commit their energy to bettering the suburbs. However, no single want or desire from any particular group or segment of our population should establish the direction for our city. Charlotte is greater than the sum of the individual challenges it faces. Since our focus should be on the greater good of the community at large, the decisions that lie ahead should not be seen as "either/or" but rather "both/and" propositions. What's good for downtown is good for the outer reaches of the city and vice versa. In this context, the real question becomes one of timing rather than need, particularly given the City's current financial situation. We must wisely plan for our future and then be patient as we work to bring the strategy to reality.

The great cities of the world evolved organically at a steady, deliberate pace over many decades. The physical environment was built to answer the practical needs of the inhabitants. Charlotte's Center City has matured to this state of organic development, thanks in large part to the thousands of new residents living in the urban core. But because Charlotte's Center City is the heart of our region's economic, cultural and entertainment activity, it must continue to reach out to citizens beyond I-277. People are naturally skeptical of narrowly focused agendas and are generally reticent to quickly accept changes imposed upon them. As with individuals, decisions cannot be forced on an entire citizenry with the expectation of immediate, unilateral acceptance.

The days of a small group of business leaders or backroom politicians making the critical decisions for Charlotte are in the past. Therefore, we must establish a different type of decision-making process. We each have the responsibility to see that Charlotte grows as one unified city, not as a loose alliance of inward-looking neighborhoods. The goal need not and should not be absolute consensus but rather a thorough understanding, through honest dialogue, of the concerns and viewpoints of our diverse and ever-evolving population. The characteristics of each of us, our various cultural, political, geographic, racial, professional and educational backgrounds and experiences, capture who we are today as a city. We, as individuals, give our city attitude and soul, something unique to Charlotte. Let us embrace and celebrate the potential of who we are collectively and continue to strive for excellence in Charlotte's future. ⏻

FIVE MEMOS FOR THE NEXT WAVE

BY DAVID WAGNER, AIA, PRINCIPAL, WAGNER MURRAY ARCHITECTS

OCTOBER 2004

A few years ago, I served as a citizen participant in crafting the 2010 Center City Vision Plan. I suggested that we use nouns to define the urban experience rather than emphasizing process when creating our vision. I suggested "memory" as a most appropriate word. I would now like to add a few more nouns to the lexicon of our planning model and nurture the possibilities and potential hidden in these words.

While graciously admitting a debt to the great Italian storyteller, Italo Calvino, I challenge us to stretch our imaginations. Calvino was drafting, "Six Memos for the Next Millennium," which was to be the Charles Elliot Norton lectures at Harvard University, when he unexpectedly died. He completed five of the six memos. Calvino was pointing out universal values for future generations. They were *lightness*, *quickness*, *exactitude*, *visibility* and *multiplicity*. I believe we can make an argument for direct organic comparisons to our city from these qualities.

First, *lightness*, in the act of writing, is removing weight, as if to say, the burden of living bedevils our desire to act with spontaneity. In city planning, weight is over-management of desires based on a false assumption of needs. Beyond an overall organizational concept, cities become light when "imagination flourishes."

Quickness, in literature, is the connection revealed between people, events and objects, each of which can become a special force. Therefore, quickness has much to do with expectations and is not necessarily measured by a string of events. A well-placed, well-designed edifice creates an urgency, which can often result in a visual rhythm of buildings and places appearing as though instantaneous, like street vendors clustered around a busy intersection.

The ancient Egyptians, as Calvino pointed out, used feathers as a counterweight on scales for the weighing of souls. Thus, *exactitude* defines a well-calculated plan of work, balanced with clear, incisive and memorable visual images. Here we can easily derive an analogy regarding the exactitude of cities. It is precisely this notion of balance which, when misconceived, leads to the banality of the urban environment. When well-defined master plans are deemed the general solution to all design issues, the reality, or should I say, the exactitude of great cities, is based not on general solutions, but on a multitude of particular solutions that lead to a general solution. Therefore, an almost imperceptible weight, when balanced against an array of visual imagery, leaves the indelible impression we call visual memory.

Calvino stated that there are two types of imaginative processes. One that starts with a word and arrives at a visual image and one that starts with an image and arrives at a word. He was describing *visibility*. Most cities are first images in our minds, followed by words to describe them when they meet our imagined expectations. Visibility then is the act of making a context, layering detail and form, and creating variety and place.

Finally, *multiplicity* is described by Calvino as a vast network of connections and events between people, places and activities. It is a notion that the world is a system of possibilities, a layer of conditions inter-related. As a composition, a city is a record of learning or knowledge, past and present. A city is a combination of experiences which tie the emotion of the moment to the memory of the place.

What does this mean for Charlotte? I think it means romance, falling in love with our city. Describing it as you would a good friend, with loquaciousness, feeling and memory. As Andrew Saint, the British historian observed, "Great cities draw us romantically toward them." ⏻

FAVORITE THINGS
April 2004

MAY 2005

I am astounded at the number of people I meet who have moved to Charlotte without a job, no ties to the City, the Carolinas, or even the South. More impressive is that once people settle here, they then convince family and friends to also move here. Charlotte has a lot to offer from a vibrant Center City and great neighborhoods, to a strong quality of life and many job opportunities. However, newcomers, as well as natives, don't often realize what it has taken for Charlotte to evolve into such a dynamic city.

Just looking back 10 years:

· Charlotte-Douglas International Airport was an international airport mostly in name only. Now, we have an international concourse that supports 1.3 million passengers and direct flights to 25 international destinations.

· Charlotte was not known as a Headquarters City, and now we are in the Top 5 of cities with Headquarters operations for Fortune 500 companies. More impressive is that 100,000 jobs have been created over the past 10 years.

· Center City was a ghost town after 5:00 p.m. and on the weekends. Now, Center City is thriving with 8,500 residents and more to come.

· Earle Village, Dalton Village, and Fairview Homes were havens for drugs and substandard housing. Now, they are neighborhoods where families can prosper.

· Billboards were placed in residential neighborhoods, brownfields added to the blight of industrial areas, sidewalks were not required, bikeways did not exist, and our tree canopy was not adequately protected. Now, we are recognized as one of the "Most Livable Cities" in America.

• Our murder rate in 1993 claimed 122 victims, and now we have almost cut that in half to 66 homicides in 2003.

• The Charlotte Trolley was a small grassroots effort. Our bus system was haphazard and didn't meet the transportation needs of our citizens. A 25-year transportation plan was only an unfunded dream, but now we are embarking on our first light rail line.

The rise of Charlotte has not been by accident, but by the hard work of thousands of Charlotteans.

Now we must look ahead to the next decade and beyond, and engage even more people to be a part of Charlotte's success story. There has been a lot of energy around attracting and engaging the 22 – 44 age group. I support those efforts and believe we have a vision that all age groups can endorse and build upon.

The vision is that Charlotte is a welcoming city and we embrace everyone, but with the opening of our arms, we have one expectation, and that is for every citizen (and business) to be involved in the community. Community involvement can include volunteering on a local neighborhood association, serving on a city board, helping a favorite charity, or joining the Chamber of Commerce (for businesses). I believe this vision is timeless and the peer pressure it has instilled is healthy.

Looking forward, we must continue to think long-term and implement the vision to address such issues as:

• Gangs. They are now prevalent in Charlotte, and we must address the need to find more positive role models for our youth.

• Corridor Revitalization. We must expand the success of South End farther down South Boulevard and to the North Tryon Street corridor. We also need to work to make Independence Boulevard a grand boulevard that not only moves traffic, but enhances the surrounding neighborhoods and businesses.

• Environment, particularly given our recent non-attainment designation for air quality. We have to provide options for people to get around the region without always using a car. We also need to strengthen our efforts to protect open space and safeguard our drinking water.

• And lastly, we can never take for granted the needs of our citizens, particularly the need to maintain a solid job base in the City of Charlotte.

While there is still much work ahead, we can take pride in how far Charlotte has come in the past decade. By capitalizing on our progress and recruiting others to join in the future success of the City, Charlotte will appeal to more newcomers, but also remain the place natives are proud to call home. ⏻

Q&A with Suzanne Fetscher

By Mark Peres

April 2004

Suzanne Fetscher is President of the McColl Center of Visual Art at 721 North Tryon Street. Originally built in 1926, the McColl Center is located in a former Associate Reformed Presbyterian Church. The McColl Center opened in 1999 as an urban artists' community.

What is the McColl Center of Visual Art?

The McColl Center is an artist-in-residence program and gallery. Artists come from all over the world to live and work in Charlotte for three months. They use our outstanding and beautiful facility like a laboratory to conduct research and create new work. We have an extraordinary facility with many specialized studios: wood, sculpture, metal, printmaking and ceramics studios, a darkroom and a digital lab.

How are artists selected?

The artists-in-residence are selected primarily because of the excellence of their work. We attempt to get a mix of emerging and mid-career artists and variety of disciplines represented in each residency session. In our selection process, we try to utilize the facility by identifying artists in as many disciplines as possible. We also attempt to have international artists-in-residence as well as regional and national artists. Approximately 50 nominators from around the world assist in identifying talent. Applications are gathered. Half of our artists are selected by a jury. The other half is selected by our senior staff to round out the field.

How is the McColl Center different from other artist-in-residence programs?

There are approximately 80 artist-in-residency programs in the U.S. Most of them are rural retreats. The McColl Center is one of a dozen programs that are urban. Our goal is to provide an opportunity for artists to connect with one another and to our community.

How does Charlotte benefit?

Our artists interact with the community in formal and informal ways. Each artist presents at least two outreaches into schools, universities and cultural and non-cultural institutions. In this way, we try to share these very talented artists with the broader public. We also have an exhibition program that is designed to showcase a range of contemporary art. We feel that the experience of having artists here for three months enriches all of us and, over time, will help shape Charlotte. Already, the McColl Center has had 100 artists in its short history. ⏻

NEVER FORGET

BY ANGELA LINDSAY, CHARLOTTE VIEWPOINT COLUMNIST

MARCH 2006

Cities are defined in large part by all of the people and events that helped shape it throughout history. The City of Charlotte has a fascinating story, and each chapter is important to understanding how it came to be. There is an ongoing event in Charlotte that is trying to keep alive a certain chapter of our city's past. As part of a leadership training class that I attend, I had the opportunity to learn about some special people who helped shape the city and unearth many little-known facts that make up the sprawling metropolis we now call Charlotte.

I am still amazed at what I learned on the 8th annual Charlotte Black Heritage Tour and Pilgrimage. Even as a native of Charlotte, most of the information that was shared was eye-opening news to me, and many of the over fifty sites I visited I did not know existed. In three hours, I took a voyage through 250 years worth of people and places, exploring the connections between this city's development and its rich black history.

The Tour documented the impact of black people on the development of Charlotte from the very origin of our nickname "The Queen City"– named after Queen Charlotte, whose ancestry is traced to the black branch of a royal Portuguese family (even Mecklenburg County was named after the German city in which she was born) – to the contributions of business merchant Alexander Carr, whose historic home on the corner of McDowell and 5th Streets was restored and now houses several law offices.

Many of the city's creative endeavors, such as the shield seen on various buildings and statues in Uptown and the creation of the Martin Luther King statue in Memorial Park, were the work of black artists. Accompanied by the insightful commentary and bottomless knowledge of our charismatic tour guide, the past came to life as sounds from the native land were channeled through an entertaining and informative African drumming display. Yet sometimes when we dredge up the past, the findings are not so pleasant. Parts of Charlotte's past are no exception.

The sting of how slaves were regarded as second class citizens was palpable during a presentation given in the balcony of a prominent church, the only place slaves were allowed to sit. Most people in the tour group were incensed by the blatant use of the innocuous term "servant" versus the more accurate description of "slave" on all the slave grave markers throughout the city (with the exception of the plot in the preserved McCoy family cemetery), and others were intrigued by the designation on a particular headstone of a slave owner's "real" daughter versus the one of a daughter he fathered illegitimately with his slave. But we were all astonished at the amount of this city's history that we as a well-educated group had never been taught and were only now learning.

I attended grade and high school in Charlotte (though not in CMS schools), but I wish that a more complete history of the City of Charlotte had somehow been a mandatory part of my curriculum. The tour, in particular, would be a valuable educational tool for students today. As a resident and particularly as a native of Charlotte, such little-known information about our city like that unearthed on the tour is important for creating more knowledgeable citizens who may even manage to become better connected as a result.

I found it fitting that I experienced this tour during the month of February, which is nationally recognized as Black History Month. But clearly Charlotte's local black history can be seen and felt year-round and continues to be created every day. The information gained from the tour is something that all Charlotteans, not just black residents, can benefit from learning about.

In our effort to lunge into a more modernized and progressive future, remnants of our city's past can, and, in many cases have been, torn down, neglected, and even altered. Therefore, it is a good idea to take a step back in time every now and then. Preserving and teaching Charlotte's true history to future generations is the only reliable way to ensure that it is never forgotten. But we all must learn exactly what that history is first. ⏻

History + Street Life = Soul

By Dan Levine, President, Levine Properties

June 2004

The Center City is the crown jewel of Charlotte. Over the years, our community has made great commitments to make the Center City the destination of choice for the arts, sports, conventions, government and business, education and entertainment. Our citizens have great pride in what the city is becoming. With all our progress, however, a central question remains: Have we created a place that calls for people to visit and return?

Great cities have it all. Chicago, New York, San Francisco, Boston, Paris and London: These are destinations that people from around the world are passionate to visit time and time again. Why? These cities have histories that are cherished and celebrated. They are places that have developed and changed incrementally over long periods of time. It is time that develops the patina of cities, and, in turn, makes them seem and feel authentic.

These cities have something special…a soul.

Charlotte's Center City has character, but does it have a soul? I submit that we are at a watershed moment in our city's history. Over the next two years, we will witness the opening of new institutions that will make great strides in transforming the soul of our city.

Johnson & Wales University opens this fall with a class of 1,200 freshmen. Think about that. Given that our current Uptown population is about 9,000, these students will increase the population by 15% overnight! More importantly, these young people will change the dynamics of the streets. In great cities, life happens on the streets, and we will see this occur with greater momentum by virtue of J&W's arrival.

The opening of the new Charlotte Arena will have an equal, yet different, impact. The Arena will host more than 40 games and another 160 events per year, bringing hundreds of thousands of people per year to our Center City. This will require a greatly expanded entertainment and restaurant district to accommodate them. The Arena's synergistic pull will reposition the social center of the region to the Center City.

These are two big, and warmly welcomed, changes that will add great pace, and momentum, to our Center City. Yet will these developments bring any more soul? The law of unintended consequences will prove over time that these monolithic projects will spawn smaller multidimensional places of personality and character.

In this very way, First Ward has the opportunity to add to the richness of our city. Our company, Levine Properties, will be involved in helping to create a 24/7 neighborhood filled with street level retail and a collection of mid-rise residential buildings. We believe in the concept of incremental development over time.

The evolution of our city's soul requires granular, unique, quirky places that cater to all people living, working and visiting the Center City. Charlotte has made great strides and has the foundation in place to grow into one of the nation's great cities...with a soul. ⏻

Charlotte raises her sword

Mordor falls

Panthers prowl

CHARLOTTE'S EMERGING BRAND
BY CHARLIE ELBERSON, PRESIDENT, ELBERSON PARTNERS

MARCH 2005

We're told Charlotte needs a message. When young residents are asked "What IS Charlotte?," they fumble to answer. The cry often heard, again rises: "Let's brand Charlotte!"

And why not? Brands are everywhere. *Wired* Magazine reported that 5,000 new brands were introduced last year. Yet the average person can name barely a few. And that's part of the problem – branding is simple in theory, but very difficult in execution.

Brands have been around for centuries. Ever since craftsmen like Paul Revere began to put a distinctive mark on their wares (thus "branding" them), brand names have been equated with value.

Functional products lend themselves easily to branding – it's why the first packaged brands were for things like cough drops. More abstract and arcane entities are harder to brand. This is why multinational conglomerates tend to select "Unisys"-style monikers and generic corporate imagery when describing themselves.

Cities that desire to market themselves often struggle with how to fit their messages under a common brand umbrella. And, because branding requires a single-minded focus, applied consistently over time, branding a city is often more frustrating than fruitful.

The branding process can explain why. A simple six-step example of the branding process might look like this:

1. Discover how customers/prospects perceive you and the universe within which you operate.
2. Compare the above to your goals, i.e. what you want to become in the long run.
3. Devise succinct, simple statements that integrate the two.
4. Evaluate statements with stakeholders and get buy-in for the one that best exemplifies the brand – called the brand premise.
5. Establish traits that reinforce and support this premise – we call this brand character or brand story.
6. Consistently and cohesively apply in all communications. Over time, brand association and perceived value will grow.

It's not hard to see why municipalities like Charlotte struggle so with branding. I've had the task of branding Charlotte before and it's not easy. (My firm developed the "What We Dream We Do" campaign a few years back.) Grabbing hold of what this city is, focusing it, and hanging on is like trying to unhook a just-landed fish – slippery and prickly at the same time.

Who are our customers and prospects? What do our customers and prospects think of us? What are our goals? Who are the stakeholders? How can we hope for buy-in? Ask these questions in Charlotte and get a million different answers, depending on who, and when, you ask.

Still, lots of U.S. cities are "branded," meaning they are already associated with a certain premise or character traits. Here are some examples:

Cities associated with single industries: D.C., Orlando, Las Vegas, Detroit, Charleston, Nashville
Cities with notable perceived physical characteristics: San Francisco, Chicago, Charleston, Miami, New York, Phoenix
Cities with universal historical significance: Boston, Philadelphia, Charleston, Richmond
Cities linked to food (and beverage): Buffalo, Memphis, New York, Philadelphia, Kansas City, Chicago, Milwaukee, Boston, San Francisco, New Orleans
Cities with attitude: New York, LA, New Orleans, San Antonio, Seattle, San Francisco, San Diego, Boston, Miami

As you scan this list observe one thing. All the brand elements: the industries, the physical characteristics, the attitude, the culture – all the above singularities are more or less organic to their communities. Some, like San Antonio, embrace their brand associations. Others talk around theirs (go to Nashville's Chamber website and try to find the phrase, "Music City.")

The fact that a city's brand association tends to form around organic factors explains in part why the branding conversation for Charlotte has been unproductive so far. Frankly, it's premature. We forget how young, as a city, Charlotte really is. We're all excited about what Charlotte can become and frustrated it's not there yet. A young sentiment about a young city.

Myself, I think Charlotte's true brand is just starting to emerge. And it will happen organically, not something we fabricate. Time and the caring hands of people who want their home to become something worthwhile still have a lot to do. But, like the father who one day notices his little girl has grown up to become a remarkable and complete woman, ready for her coronation, Charlotte's about to show us what she'll be when she grows up. I intend to help her all I can. ⏻

Q&A with Tom Low
By Mark Peres

July 2005

Tom Low, AIA, is an architect and town planner, and serves as Director of the Charlotte regional office of Duany Plater-Zyberk & Company (DPZ). DPZ is widely recognized as being at the vanguard of the "New Urbanism" movement as a counter to the proliferation of suburban sprawl. Tom, a native of Roanoke, moved to Charlotte in 1979 after graduating with a Bachelor in Architecture from Virginia Tech. Tom later received his Master of Architecture from the University of Miami with a specialization in Town Design. Tom opened an office for DPZ in Charlotte in 1995, and is actively involved with design and development projects, research, and education within North and South Carolina. He recently founded the Civic by Design Forum, a citizen-centered forum focused on the quality of life and built environment of the Charlotte region.

Tell us about the Civic by Design Forum.
We started it with support from the Charlotte AIA and the Levine Museum of the New South. The mission of the Charlotte Region Civic by Design Forum is to elevate the quality of the Charlotte region's built environment and to promote public participation in the creation of a more beautiful and functional region for all. We discuss a wide range of topics, from urban infill, what makes for great streets, affordable housing, open spaces, transit and civic infrastructure, to growth and physical design. We are a non-profit group with a board of directors and steering committee. The forum is free and open to the public. We meet the second Tuesday of every month from 5:30 - 6:30 p.m. at the Levine Museum of the New South, 200 East Seventh Street.

Why did you start it?

Every area where people live has a regime in control. In New York, it might be City Hall and Wall Street. In Portland, it might be powerful environmental coalitions. In Richmond and Charleston, traditional Old South cities, it might be an old social establishment. In New South cities, like Atlanta, Houston, Dallas and Charlotte, the controlling regime is developers. The personality of each city is usually an extension of the personality of the controlling regime. Like other New South cities, Charlotte is business and future-oriented, open to newcomers, and less concerned with design, creativity and the arts (unless it's good for business and development). We're beginning to see a broadening in our civic personality as we begin to embrace design for its intrinsic value. We saw an opportunity to bring citizens together to talk about design and creativity, and influence the qualitative aspects of city life. Our approach is holistic and cross-disciplinary. We modeled it after the Nashville Civic Design Center, which has had great success bringing design professionals and non-professional residents together to impact the city's physical environment.

How does the Civic by Design model work?

There are many well-intentioned organizations trying to promote smart growth. Most of them work independently and do not actively cooperate. Some take a planning department approach. Others follow a university educational model. Each has its own constituency, funding sources and particular agendas. Our approach is to offer a place and process for these different interests to inform each other, and to have as a result, a stronger say for design. We follow an "open space technology" process to help participants share concerns and suggestions on issues. We capture insights and suggestions. As we evolve, and have a better understanding of priorities and our own sustainable capabilities, we will take more action-oriented steps to influence civic design choices.

What civic design issue is of particular interest to you?

I'm interested in regional scale and new town planning connected to our transportation interchanges. We have focused a lot of due energy on the Center City, and on the whole, it seems that the Center City is on its way to becoming a thriving urban space. Architects and planners, developers, citizens and politicians, roughly in that order, have gotten it: We want an urban core with great street life, open green spaces, mixed use at various price points, and a flow of people and ideas that is porous between edges. What we haven't focused on is containing the edges of the region. The I-485 beltway is a huge development catalyst. For the most part, what we build around each interchange of our transportation network is crud. It's really awful, car-centric sprawl, and we all know it. But it doesn't have to be that way. Just like we have brought better design to the inner city, we can bring better design to the outer city. New towns with walkable main streets are planned all the time. We need to plan and build compact, connected, human scale towns at our interchanges. We could reduce car trips by as much as two-thirds, which would be a massive environmental benefit on a regional scale, let alone turning awful places into interesting places to work and live. With I-485 not yet complete, Charlotte has an opportunity to become a national leader in interchange town planning and design. ⏻

CHARLOTTE, GREATER AND MORE BEAUTIFUL
BY SUSAN BURGESS, CHARLOTTE CITY COUNCIL MEMBER, AT-LARGE

DECEMBER 2004

Greetings from Indianapolis, where I am attending the National League of Cities annual conference and really paying attention to the details of this meeting. Next year around this time, 7,000 City Council members and mayors from all over the nation will convene in Charlotte. From my Indy hotel window, I see a beautiful, vibrant Center City, with museums, a large retail mall, facilities for every conceivable professional sport, a large convention center, old important-looking government buildings, many other restored buildings, parks, and interesting, inspiring public art. Monuments are everywhere, commemorating people and events meaningful to these Hoosiers. I'm told there are more monuments here than any American city, except for Washington, D.C. I like them. I also see lots of people dashing around day and night in the cold misty wind, colorful scarves blowing behind them.

I try to imagine what my colleagues will see next year during their visit to the Queen City. Our Center City is vibrant, too, with probably more residential, but much less retail; more shiny new buildings, but less preserved history than Indianapolis. We have museums like Discovery Place, which is, as much as I love it, beginning to be a little outdated; our new awesome arena; churches; underused and undersized parks; and hopefully, clear Carolina blue skies. What is missing in our city is public art that is fun, memorable and that adds color, interest and maybe a little funkiness. This gap is something we will have an opportunity to fill if we stay firm to our commitment to the 1% set-aside for public art.

In 2003, the Charlotte City Council passed a policy that committed 1% of the budgets of publicly funded projects to the creation and installation of public art. The vote was unanimous and celebrated. The process adopted was one that attempts to keep politics and politicians out of the selection to avoid the "Gumby" debacle of the 1980s, when radio disc jockeys ridiculed the Joel Shapiro sculpture selected by the Arts and Science Council to be placed at the Charlotte Coliseum. The City Council at the time intervened and killed the Shapiro project, which was ultimately replaced by round holly bushes. Joel Shapiro has since become a renowned sculptor, whose Coliseum work would have quadrupled in value and would have most probably been moved to our new arena. The Public Arts Commission, made up of art-savvy volunteers and appointed by the Mayor and Council, is charged with the selection and contracting with artists to invest our 1% set-aside.

This arrangement has worked swimmingly until Mayor McCrory decided he didn't like the Andrew Leicester work commissioned for the new arena by the Public Arts Commission. After instructing the Chair of the Commission not to sign any more contracts, he added the entire program to our agenda for review. Of course, the Mayor has no power to intervene in a Council-approved process, but he does indeed have the power to add the issue to the agenda, so the whole public art issue is now again before us, unfortunately. I am hopeful that our citizens will encourage the City Council to "stay the course" in our commitment to public art. This commitment is essential for Charlotte to mature into a beautiful, progressive city.

Not only do we need new public art, we need a more comprehensive, long-range arts and culture vision and plan to fund, build, manage and enjoy this aspect of our city life. The Cultural Arts Task Force will soon report their recommendations for our city to do just that. I encourage all of our citizens to join the Council in studying options and embracing a commitment to implement our plan.

This morning the president of the National League of Cities, Charlie Lyons, gave his swan song speech. He ended it with the words of the Athenian Code. I believe its words hold relevance in our city today. So repeat after me,

"We will never bring disgrace on this our City by an act of dishonesty or cowardice. We will fight for the ideals and Sacred Things of the City both alone and with many…. We will strive increasingly to quicken the public's sense of civic duty. Thus in all these ways we will transmit this City, not only not less, but greater and more beautiful than it was transmitted to us." ⏻

And the Walls Came Tumbling Down

By Christa Wagner, Charlotte ViewPoint Columnist

July 2005

*H*uman industry has been in full swing for little over a century, yet it has brought about a decline in almost every ecosystem on the planet. Nature doesn't have a design problem. People do.

– William McDonough, architect and designer

In economics, we learn that efficiency is important. That's why companies are always emphasizing the bottom line. When it comes to infrastructure, an important part of a company's fixed costs, it would make sense to use the most efficient building techniques and design to save money over the building's life. Yet most companies shy away from these innovative practices because of presumed increases in upfront costs.

Then there's the strategy of "build and run," favored by such pitiless outfits as big-box retailers, which amounts to buying the right to build, conquer and leave the fallout to the vanquished.

I would never suggest that Charlotte runs the business of being a city the way a strip-mall promoter runs its operation. But there is a troubling similarity in Charlotte's zeal for abandoning buildings before the end of their natural life (or designing them for short, undistinguished lives to begin with).

It's puzzling how Charlotte can afford so much demolition and renovation. Consider several recent examples. Charlotte's original coliseum was built on East Independence in 1955. In 1988, a new coliseum was built on Tyvola Road, with multiple lanes for shuttling traffic from centrally located neighborhoods where most people lived) to the middle of nowhere (that is, until the coliseum was built). Now a new arena, this one in the Center City, is scheduled for completion in 2006.

Charlotte's first Convention Center, located Uptown, looked like a Soviet-era factory, lacking street-level windows, doors and a reason for remaining operational for more than a quarter of a century. A new Convention Center opened in 1995. The original Convention Center was demolished at 7:30 a.m. on Sunday, June 26th.

Then there was City Fair, an Uptown megaplex with retail and restaurants, which lasted less than five years.

Why is Charlotte so uninterested in building to last? Of course, I don't have the answer. But my clever dad, who happens to be an architect, offered the following explanation. He cut to the chase: "A number of buildings constructed in recent decades, public and private, were banal," he says. "While we don't miss the buildings, we may miss their intended purposes."

So, of course, we build them all over again.

And while one can imagine the incentive an architect might have to encourage tearing down and starting all over (more money), there is a greater incentive in building it right the first time (more legacy).

My dad agrees: "A well-designed building is a building that is meant to be used for many generations," he says. "When you look at the Charlotte Convention Center destroyed after 25 years, you need to start questioning the sustainability and longevity of our built environment."

I'm questioning already. In my day job, I work for the Sierra Club, the nation's oldest grassroots environmental advocacy organization. Our local group of volunteers successfully encouraged the City of Charlotte to invest in hybrid-electric technology for its municipal fleet. We gained bipartisan support on the City Council and delivered hundreds of signed "green fleet" petitions from constituents to City Hall.

And to answer every economist's pressing concern, the City took this innovative step because it's cost-effective. You know, efficient. Hybrid cars cost less at the pump and cost less to maintain. Charlotte plans to add 14 hybrids next year and looks forward to a decade of savings in the hundreds of thousands of dollars, not to mention the benefits for air quality.

Hybrid cars are futuristic and cool. They use fewer raw materials, like oil; they're economically stimulating because the demand for them is so high; they reduce global warming and therefore help protect the planet; and, because of the oil thing, hybrids could help defuse tense geo-political relationships.

Wow. If a well-designed car can do all of this, imagine what a well-designed basketball arena, or a convention center or a retail/restaurant megaplex, or a library or an office building or a Wal-Mart could do and mean. ⏻

Favorite Things
December 2005

Charlotte: A Commitment to Neighborhoods & Urban Revitalization

By Darrel Williams, Sr., FAIA, Principal, Neighboring Concepts

February 2006

Over the past 25 years, Charlotte has done a great job preserving and revitalizing many of its finest neighborhoods. While there is still much work to do, Charlotte is the envy of other cities throughout the country relative to its commitment and investment throughout many of these communities. Some of these neighborhoods, which are located within a three-mile radius of the Center City, are precious remnants of streetcar suburbs. Charlotte's success is also a result of its corporate support, strong business community and clean government.

Despite what has been done, there is still much work to do. However, it will require a commitment beyond what government can do. These neighborhoods reflect the range in economic and social challenges that are apparent throughout America. While many areas hardly experience any social challenges, since the years of urban renewal, several of them suffer poorer health, fewer successful small businesses, crime, violence and fragmented families. How much of that is the result of the dispersion and destruction created by urban renewal? What would it mean for all citizens to live in safe neighborhoods where they can walk to a store, to church or to work with trees and greenery, with a range of small businesses that employ neighborhood adolescents and where people know and trust one another?

Across this country, in the years between urban renewal and the birth of mega shopping centers, we lost one inner city neighborhood after another. The bulldozers destroyed much more than physical structures. With the past destruction of the Brooklyn neighborhood in Second Ward, Charlotte was no exception. Urban neighborhoods of our childhood like Brooklyn had distinct rhythms, relationships, flavors and aromas. They included people of all ages and incomes. Residents in Brooklyn understood the significance of the barber and beauty shop – much more than a place to get a hair cut! They knew that the local soul food restaurant was as much about who was there and the bonds that were forged as the goodness of the food that was served. They were community! Like other cities, Charlotte has learned from the mistakes of its past.

In recent years, it has become increasingly evident that people of all ethnic, social and economic levels yearn for the neighborhoods of their childhood of the '50s and '60s. From the west coast to the east coast, downtown areas are being reclaimed with new housing and mixed-use public-private development projects. These trends, along with billions of dollars being spent on alternative modes of transportation, new infrastructure and land use plans are bringing deserved attention to urban neighborhoods on the fringes of America's central cities, and Charlotte is no exception. With rising fuel prices, the costs of commuting and time spent to and from the suburbs, along with better understanding the real purchasing power and economic potential of central city neighborhoods, the real estate and development community is starting to see the light.

The "new urban residential towers" currently underway in Uptown are largely succeeding in bringing vibrancy and real life to our Center City. This resurgence of new residents will help fill the gaps that are generally missing in most downtown areas and help influence some major retail in the Center City. While the new urban towers bring vibrancy and life to the Center City, we must be cautious about creating vertical versions of the gated communities that continue to rise up in the suburbs – notably devoid of that human interaction and neighborhood character that is the foundation of community. Also, we must ensure that the economic development opportunities in the Center City do not end at Brookshire Freeway and I-77.

Rising fuel prices and increasing commute times make these neighborhoods vulnerable to vertical urban sprawl that rips out the heart and soul of urban neighborhoods. Government cannot attain the balance between new development and urban revitalization alone. Preserving diversity – economic, cultural, racial, and age – is a challenge to be met by the public and private sectors working cooperatively and intentionally with existing residents. Vibrant urban neighborhoods are successful because of the shared history and experience and interaction of those who live and work and play in them – not simply a visual return to the past. Diversity is our history, our power and strength. ⏻

Q&A with Mollie Faison

By Mark Peres

November 2004

Mollie Faison serves on the Board of Directors of Brookstone Schools, a faith-based "school of academic excellence" that serves low-income, inner-city youth in Charlotte. Mollie has been active in Charlotte philanthropy for many years, serving in several leadership roles, including as the project chair of Queen's Table, which brought the four sculptures representing Charlotte history to the Square.

Tell us about Brookstone Schools.

Brookstone Schools is projected as a K-8 academy serving the most at-risk children in our community. We saw a need to rigorously educate and inspire children who live in severely challenged neighborhoods within the inner-core of Charlotte. These children have traditionally not performed well in school and have not contributed to society, largely because of family ills and social decay. Many people believe the challenge of educating these children is insurmountable. We disagree. We believe every child can learn and contribute positively to society. Brookstone Schools is now in its fourth year of academic excellence, equipping low-income students for future leadership and service.

How and when did the school come about in Charlotte?

It started as an idea eight years ago. Noah Manyika, a pastor from Zimbabwe, came to Charlotte with a calling to start a school that served very poor, inner-city, disadvantaged youth. The school would help heal and stabilize at-risk neighborhoods. He gathered a core group of volunteers and donors who saw his vision. The school was named Brookstone from the biblical story of David who gathered five stones from a brook and used one to slay Goliath. In this case, the founders sought to slay the myth that these students could not consistently perform at high academic levels and lead their communities. In 2000, the school started with 16 children in kindergarten and first grade. A class has been added every year. Brookstone now has 73 children who are consistently performing at or above grade level.

How is Brookstone educating its students?

The school follows the core knowledge curriculum of the University of Virginia. The school provides expert direct instruction with an emphasis on mastery and goal-setting, with no more than 15 students per classroom. Brookstone has high expectations, demands personal accountability and offers early training in leadership and service. The school emphasizes values and manners and offers love.

How does Brookstone Schools benefit Charlotte?

All great schools nurture productive citizens who come into leadership. Great schools create community. Brookstone is unique in that it is a privately funded school that is lifting up the most disadvantaged students in our city. The school creates a centrifugal force of positive transformation that changes the lives of families and children.

How can citizens help Brookstone succeed?

The school is entirely dependent on the generosity of citizens. The school needs financial support and volunteers to secure its foundation. School leaders would be happy to visit individuals, clubs and organizations to share the vision. We invite the active contribution of those committed to the education and well-being of at-risk children in Charlotte. ⏻

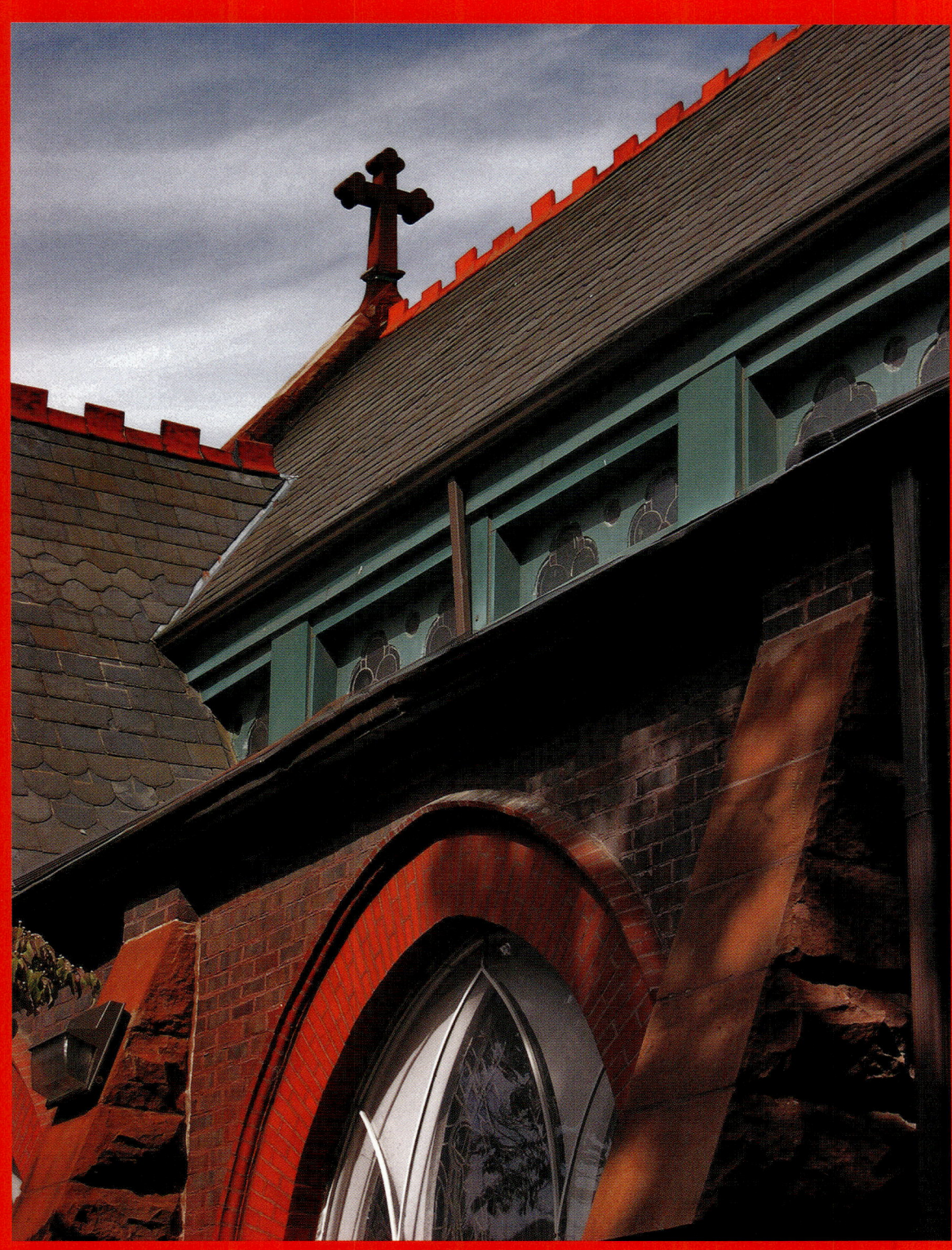

REPORTING THE NEWS

BY ROGER SAROW, PRESIDENT & GENERAL MANAGER, WFAE 90.7FM

JULY 2006

It takes nerve to operate a service that ticks people off. Now and then I hear from a listener who is positively outraged about a story heard on WFAE, either a locally originated piece or a story produced by one of our networks, such as NPR. Certainly there are instances when listeners are rightfully indignant at our content. Editors and reporters simply make mistakes. Beyond that, reporters can oversimplify a story. At other times radio professionals are guilty of haste in reporting, bias or paltry fact checking. All of those situations warrant a listener's agitation.

I see an increasing incidence, however, of listeners who complain simply because they disagree with a story, and therefore feel empowered to demand that the story be yanked off the air (and the offending reporter yanked by the neck). It reminds me of an NPR interview with a British journalist shortly before the U.S. invasion of Iraq. The skeptical writer said, "You Yanks are not really interested in hearing facts these days; you're interested in reassurance."

Maybe this is a core failing of today's customer-focused media: we start to assume that the basic content of the news we consume should be pleasant and reassuring, rather than upsetting or disquieting. I see this as an interesting paradox in on-line news and commentary. When you can receive the news topics you desire – how you want it, when you want it – whose job is it to set your teeth on edge? Can a democracy move forward when citizens can pick and choose their individual realities?

Are traditional reporters simply watching out for their economic backsides when they advocate an editorial function in news gathering?

You won't be shocked to hear that I support the role of public interest, non-commercial American media as a gap filler and conscience tweaker. Public radio stations all across the nation aggregate funds from their local markets in order to produce long-form national and world news. They do so at a time when most commercial television networks have drastically trimmed their international news staffing.

On the other hand, public stations are misinformed if they take a holier-than-thou posture toward their commercial news colleagues, or certainly if they look down their noses at their audiences. Many public stations are serving the public well by taking a longer view in their programming. They are concentrating on the long-term intellectual and civic well-being of their communities, even as their commercial media colleagues face relentless pressure from Wall Street to turn in a string of climbing quarterly profits.

A complaint often heard is that mainstream media outlets are liberal, and public broadcasters are especially flawed in this way. To paraphrase retired veteran NBC anchorman Tom Brokaw, journalism does indeed do the following: talk about the disadvantaged in the society, investigate matters of social inequality, question authority and act as a skeptic toward our government. If those are "liberal" traits, then mainstream media are guilty as charged. On the other hand, somebody ought to do this work for the good of society, and who better but writers benefiting from the protections of the First Amendment.

Ted Koppel was recently interviewed in The Wall Street Journal about his decision to provide commentary and analysis for NPR programs. He said, "NPR's leaders still believe it is the responsibility of the journalist to focus the attention of the listener on issues that are important. All too many media outlets right now think the correct way to lead is to take a poll, or study the demographics, and see what it is that the people who are most attractive to the advertisers want."

Koppel is not the only broadcast journalist with a national following to join the NPR roster. Robert Krulwish – an NPR veteran – recently left his ABC News position to return to the NPR's science beat. Editors and reporters from large daily metros have joined the NPR journalism team within the last two to three years. Cokie Roberts is credible and informative whether she's wearing her ABC or NPR hat.

Wouldn't it be nice if we, as listeners, support their work by welcoming the occasional, thoughtful challenge to our individual assumptions and value systems? Let's call it "selective discomfort" and welcome it as the next wave of interactive media. ⏻

IMAGINING CHARLOTTE
BY MARY TRIBBLE, PRESIDENT, TRIBBLE CREATIVE GROUP

JUNE 2005

Imagination can accomplish surprising things. As our company celebrates its 20th anniversary, we are exploring the concept of imagination. For us, it's usually about a client's dream for a milestone celebration, a vision to communicate appreciation to employees, or a concept to roll out a new plan in a meaningful way. The client comes to us with an idea and our staff brings its own brand of imagination to the project. The concept comes into focus, evolves and ultimately culminates in a much better project through a collaborative process.

Through that collaborative process, there are invariably differing opinions – sometimes strongly so. Perhaps I don't think a client's idea will work logistically; maybe someone on my staff thinks the creative concept could be better. In some cases, the idea is great but the proposed execution misses the mark.

Usually, though, imagination gets better with a little bit of conflict. It forces us to rethink our position, include others' suggestions and create a better product in the end.

It occurs to me that this is how great cities work, too.

Imagine a group of rebels gathered at a bar in 1775, drinking up enough courage to declare the county's independence from England. Imagine a man sitting on a patch of dirt in Concord dreaming of an oval track that would someday attract hundreds of thousands of fans and generate millions of dollars for the region. Imagine a man standing on Trade and Tryon conjuring up a 60-story office tower, innovative cultural facilities and nightlife in Uptown Charlotte. Imagine a family dreaming of the roar of a crowd at an NFL game at a state-of-the-art stadium, or a business owner dreaming of a new NBA franchise and Uptown arena.

Few of these ideas were without controversy or nay-sayers. Most people think the Mecklenburg Declaration never existed; folks dismissed NASCAR as redneck until they started calculating the economic impact. No one would have believed that the streets of Uptown Charlotte would teem with people after hours, but they do. Many thought we were a long shot for the NFL, and the Uptown arena controversy was one of the most contentious in recent Charlotte history.

Imagination drives success, but it can also spark controversy. Much of the time, the person with the big idea is the subject of derision or ridicule – or at least a little behind-the-scene jealous whispers. Many times they are challenged. But in the past, at least, Charlotte's imaginative thinkers have worked through these challenges, created compromise when necessary, and in the end, succeeded in improving our lot.

As Charlotte continues to grow, however, we sometimes indulge in so much zealous confrontation and self-gratifying scorn, that we risk quashing the imaginative spirit that's brought us so much success. The folks with the good ideas may tire of fighting their way to consensus. Or worse, the ideas could get so watered down in order to please everyone that they result in mediocrity.

I've learned in my office that for imagination to win out, you've got to create a safe place for it to be nurtured. It's that way with cities, too.

Here are some things that Charlotte should keep hold of if we're going to continue to foster imagination:

• Openness. An imaginative city must be open and tolerant to new ideas. And it needs open space – clear patches of undeveloped land where we can be inspired by nature.

• Diversity. The best ideas come from collaboration with people different than you.

• Positive energy. Political bashing, name calling and anger-driven tactics don't cultivate creative thinking.

• Compassion. An imaginative city takes care of its elderly, its children and those less fortunate, balancing unbridled growth with attention to critical services.

If we want to continue to be a great city, let's do all we can to encourage imagination. ⏻

Why Whitewater Matters
By Vic Howie, Chairman, U.S. National Whitewater Center

August 2004

I t started four years ago as an idea drawn on the back of a napkin. Soon this idea will be a reality. The U.S. National Whitewater Center will be a 307-acre outdoor adventure center providing the Charlotte region with the world's most unique outdoor recreational and environmental learning experience. There is nothing else in the world that will compare to this facility when it opens in March 2006, and this gives Charlotte a once-in-a-lifetime opportunity to create a truly unique experience!

The Center will be only 10 minutes from Uptown Charlotte, located along the Catawba River and Interstate 85 in western Mecklenburg County. Since it will be a public park, Olympic-caliber athletes, weekend warriors and casual observers will be able to share this world-class sports and training center. The masterpiece of the Center will be a 25-acre multiple channel artificial river that can be easily modified from "easy water" to more challenging rapids for all levels of rafting, canoeing and kayaking. Other sports and activities will include flat-water boating, 11 miles of mountain biking trails, an indoor-outdoor climbing facility, trail running, and a full compliment of dining options. Additionally, the Center will host the world's most innovative swift-water rescue training facility, where our own Charlotte Fire Department will train themselves and many other fire and rescue squads from around the country to save lives.

So, why does the U.S. National Whitewater Center matter and what does this mean for you? Three quick reasons are evident: 1) impact on the community, 2) economic impact, and 3) the Olympic factor.

First, the impact on the community will come in multiple ways. Most important are the youth and family activities and programming. The YMCA, Girl Scouts, Boy Scouts, Police Athletic League, Boys and Girls Clubs, schools and church groups are just some of the organizations that will benefit from programming and access to the Center. Teaching our youth the skills of whitewater paddling, climbing and mountain biking under the care of exceptional leaders will expose them to skills so necessary to succeeding in the adult world: risk assessment, teamwork, leadership, knowing when to say no, and persistence in achieving a goal. It will also be a place for our community to get out and play – for families, grandparents with grandchildren, teenage youth, singles, couples, and anyone who wants to enjoy an active, outdoor experience.

Second, the economic impact of the Center is estimated at $37 million annually. We will create 690 new jobs, provide a world-class amenity for recruiting job talent nationally, be a major tourism destination and will add an incredibly unique venue to the amenity package for luring convention business to our city. The swift water rescue business will provide a consistent need for accommodations in our hotels. National and international Olympic-caliber kayak events could bring as many as 80 countries to our city for the competition – athletes, coaches, media, and fans who will experience our city and hospitality, and spend their money here.

Topping it off is the Olympic factor. We were successful in attracting our first Olympic sport governing body, USA Canoe and Kayak (USACK). This national group, located Uptown, is now fully staffed by Charlotte-based employees and is responsible for developing our national and Olympic level athletes to compete on the world circuit. Many of these athletes will be moving here to Charlotte to live, work, go to school and train, and also to be involved in our schools and civic organizations. The Center will also be designated as a U.S. Olympic Training Facility, and will be the ONLY one in the U.S. where you can go play at a USOC training site right beside Olympic athletes.

From Day One, our founding team has stood by a dream that we feel will one day be a reality: An athlete from Charlotte will be standing on the platform in the Olympics, and with an Olympic medal around their neck, he or she will say "It all started in Charlotte." ⏻

January renewal

Plus ça change

Plus c'est la même chose

Aster, Milkweed & Mint

By Christina Ritchie, Charlotte ViewPoint Colimnist

August 2005

Think of any city, USA. What comes to mind? Sports teams? Buildings and arenas? Public transportation? Smog? Think harder…What about its ecology for civilization?

For me, cities were always the polluted, paved, anti-plant. Growing up in the farmlands of small-town New Jersey (yes, it actually exists!), my association was "Suburbs-green. City-gross." My city-wide exposure was limited, and I was happy in the woods. But, having moved to Charlotte, gained perspective, and learned that plants actually do exist in cities, I am now learning the importance of their urban presence.

Charlotte provides for a wealth of native plant species. Many people choose to invite familiars like flowering dogwood, Carolina rhododendron, or verbena into their landscaping projects. Some may seek lobelia or fringed loostrife. Fortunate backyards are graced by the presence of oak, hickory, and evergreen trees. Blackeyed susan, bee balm, and aster are often garden members. Because the aesthetic contributions of hundreds of Charlotte's native tree, shrub, plant, flower and grass species are readily apparent, their ecological significance is often overlooked.

Charlotte's native plant species evolve naturally with the changing biological and physical aspects of the region. They are thus uniquely adapted to the environment. The plants are tolerant of the region's temperature extremes, use nutrients from the soil effectively, and grow well with the amount of average rainfall. Many provide food and shelter to local animals, beneficial insects, and migratory birds. Some offer protection against invasive, introduced plant species.

The benefits of landscaping with native plants in an urban setting are vast, though two are most notable: First, the efficiency with which they are able to thrive minimizes strain on natural resources. Second, landscaping with "locals" maintains the unique character of the natural environment.

Occasionally, Charlotte's unique urban character collides with its ecological character in a beautiful way. I recommend a visit to the McGill Rose Garden. There lies a stunning example of natural beauty cultivated in the heart of an urban environment. But nearby, a more subtle example sits amid Uptown Charlotte. A butterfly garden has emerged on 9th street. The students of Trinity Episcopal School cultivated the garden on the side of the road near the entrance to the school parking lot. It is a naturally thriving, visually pleasing, ecologically sound example of pride in our natural local assets. The garden sprung from little more than a strip of grass next to the sidewalk. With some TLC and maintenance, the garden has become a home for many species of insects, butterflies, spiders and animals. Birds often pause to rest among the coneflower and milkweed. The occasional stray cat takes shelter and rests while the air above and around is constantly abuzz and aflutter.

Charlotte, as a city, is like that butterfly garden. Though residents lightheartedly note the seeming scarcity of the "native Charlottean," the natives do exist. They, like the plants, are responsible for sustaining the life and character of the city garden. A collection of aster, milkweed, mint, coneflower and verbena entices butterflies, and invites migration. Similarly, the unique composition of people in Charlotte, and the culture and history they maintain in their evolving environment, is drawing all sorts of brightly colored beings here.

A butterfly garden can be kept simple attracting just a few butterflies, or it can be quite full, with diverse plants, multiple water sources, and a mix of sunny and shady parts. Cities are very similar. Some remain relatively small, lack diversity of race, ethnicity, or ideas, and seem to be unchanging.

Charlotte is not one of these cities. It is big, and beautiful, and growing. Stated succinctly, the requirements for any successful butterfly garden are food, water, shelter and a place to lay eggs. The needs for a successful city garden begin with a similar list. But we humans are increasingly more complex. We also want jobs, schools, transportation, worship, entertainment and healthcare, to name just a few. The increasing number of individuals happily buzzing around the garden of Charlotte indicates the city's ability to furnish those requests. As our city continues to evolve, we must work to sustain the endearing character of the city as well as the natural character of its ecology. ⏻

Q&A with James Meena

By Mark Peres

June 2005

James Meena is General Director and Principal Conductor of Opera Carolina. He has led opera performances for the Pittsburgh Opera, Portland Opera, L'Opera de Montreal, Opera Lyra Ottawa, Orlando Opera, Sarasota Opera, Opera Pacific in Orange County (California), and the Utah Opera. He has had concert appearances with the Pittsburgh Symphony, National Symphony Orchestra R.O.C., the KBS Symphony in Seoul, South Korea, the Winston-Salem Symphony, the Charlotte Symphony, Egypt's Cairo Philharmonic, the Orchestra Regionale Toscana in Florence, Italy and the Teatro Massimo Bellini in Catania, Sicily. James is a native of Cleveland, and a graduate of the Carnegie Mellon University and the Baldwin Wallace College Conservatory of Music.

How would you describe Opera Carolina to someone you just met?

Opera Carolina is the largest and most successful professional opera company in the Carolinas, performing the great works of the 18th, 19th and 20th centuries. We reach 75,000 people each year with an extensive array of grand opera performances and educational programs. We join our local company with some of the greatest artists in the world who perform the major roles to present a season of exciting live opera at the Belk Theater each year.

What is the main strength of Opera Carolina? What does it do exceptionally well?

Our strength is our product. Opera Carolina is recognized for the quality of our main stage productions and the effectiveness of our educational programs. Further, we are recognized for the creativity of our marketing and audience development initiatives, which received the 2004 BOB award, and our commitment to community service.

Opera competes with new media, sports and entertainment. Why should someone spend limited discretionary money on opera?

Opera provides an entertainment option like no other. Opera is itself a combination of drama, music and spectacle that can only best be appreciated live. That is why opera audiences in Charlotte and across the country have grown steadily in the last twenty years. It has something for everyone. Plus, since we produce four operas a season, people can attend an opera without sacrificing a great deal of time or money. With ticket prices that start at $15.00, Opera Carolina is affordable to anyone.

Tell us about the new season. What should we know?

The new season features four compelling stories of four great women. *The Pearl Fishers* tells the story of a Buddhist priestess who breaks her vows so she may be with the man she loves – a timeless story wrapped in exquisite music. The season continues with our annual presentation of the Christmas favorite *Amahl & The Night Visitors* at the McGlohon Theater. Next we perform *La Traviata* – the story of Camille, which was the basis for the blockbuster movie *Pretty Woman*. It is one of the most beloved operas of all time. Then, Rossini's retelling of *Cinderella* is a touching and hilarious comedy. The season ends with a new opera by Grammy Award winning composer Richard Danielpour with a script by Pulitzer and Nobel Prize winning author Toni Morrison. The opera is *Margaret Garner*. Margaret's true story was the inspiration for Morrison's acclaimed novel *Beloved*, and is an historical drama of this fugitive slave whose sacrifice speaks to modern audiences in a way that is compelling yet beautiful.

What is your hope for the company? What is success for Opera Carolina?

As with any business, success is measured in a number of ways. We measure success by the satisfaction of our customers – audience members and community partners; ending the year with a positive financial report (which we have done 11 our of the last 12 years); a growing customer base, which we are proud to say is the case with Opera Carolina; and the knowledge that our product is the best it can be. My hope for Opera Carolina is the same that we have for greater Charlotte – that we continue to build a company of true quality that is a valued community resource for years to come. ⏻

GROWTH AND COMMUNITY

By Karen Geiger, President, Karen Geiger & Associates

APRIL 2005

In 1774, Charlotte's population was 200. In 1974 we became the nation's 50th largest city with a population that had increased a thousand-fold. Ten years ago we were at approximately 400,000, and today we are greater than half a million people. It is estimated that we will break one million by 2012. What implications might this have for our community?

Community is important to all of us in that it gives us identity, a sense of belonging and security. When it is strong, it serves to protect our freedom and motivates us to higher standards. It thrives when differences are seen as part of the whole, when leaders are capable of seeing a perspective that is broader than their own self-interest, when there is room for mavericks and nonconformists, when there is high participation from all members, when people in it have some core of shared values, and when each member of the community is respected, recognized and thanked for their hard work, and is aware that they need one another.

Growth changes the way we build community. In the traditional small community, there is homogeneity: people have many things in common and are usually alike. Conformity is usually high, and there is a sense of history. There is often a leader or group of leaders who are dominant, and the rest of the community willingly follows them. Those of us who were in Charlotte 20 years ago might describe Charlotte this way: decisions were often made by a small group of powerful businessmen, the community respected this group of "city fathers," government bodies were represented by people who focused as much on the city as a whole as well as their own district, the school system was smaller and more localized. The names McColl, Crutchfield and Lee were highly visible and most people knew who they were.

In our city of just under half a million today, we live in neighborhoods that are often homogenous within themselves: by race, income and, in some cases, political leanings. The increase in two-working-parent and single-parent families results in people not getting to know each other as well simply because there is less time together. Our sense of community often comes from our neighborhood, and our religious affiliations – where we are usually with those similar to us. The Social Capital Community Benchmark Survey done in 2000 reinforced this trend, indicating that we are high in areas where we "bond" with others like us, but low in areas where we might "bridge" to those different to us.

What does this have to do with leadership as a tool to make and keep Charlotte as the healthy community we envision? First, we must begin to view leadership as a process as much as a position. If we continue to support the model of "dominant leader/compliant follower," then we put ourselves in a less-involved position and where we depend on new highly visible leaders to emerge to tell us what to do next. What we can do instead is develop a "powerful leader/powerful follower" model. Coined by Ira Chaleff in 1995, this model assumes that leaders rarely use their power effectively over long periods unless they are supported by followers who have the stature to help them do so. In this model, we involve ourselves in the issues we care about and help the people in leadership positions to carry out the duties we have asked them to carry out.

Second, we can discipline ourselves to socialize and/or get to know people who are different than us. This prevents the human tendency to generalize and make conclusions based on limited information and gives too much power to institutions like the media to shape our opinions vs. learning from our own experience. As John Murphy said when he was our Superintendent of CMS, (my paraphrasing), "If you won't integrate yourselves in your neighborhoods, then why do you think it's hard for me to make integrated, neighborhood schools?" We set our leaders up when we ask them to represent only our homogenous interests, when the reality is that we must work as a larger, more concerted community.

Maintaining a healthy community as we grow depends on each of us being courageous followers and leaders. There is a role for everyone. ⏻

Favorite Things
July 2005

- Sonoma Modern American
- Barebones Theater Group
- City Stage 2005
- Community School of the Arts
- Banana Pudding at Simmons

Q&A with Ronnie Bryant

By Mark Peres

December 2005

Ronnie Bryant is President and CEO of the Charlotte Regional Partnership ("CRP"). The CRP is an economic development organization that promotes the 16-county Charlotte USA region as a premier location for businesses considering expansion or relocation. Prior to joining CRP, Bryant led the Pittsburgh Regional Alliance where he marketed the region and collaborated with regional economic development agencies to develop and implement job creation strategies. Before working in Pittsburgh, Bryant was the Senior Vice President of the Economic Development Division for the St. Louis Regional Chamber & Growth Association. He is a graduate of Louisiana State University and the Economic Development Institute at the University of Oklahoma in Norman. Bryant is a recipient of the American Economic Development Council's Robert B. Cassell Leadership Award for excellence in leadership.

What is the role and function of the Charlotte Regional Partnership?

The role of the CRP is to market the Charlotte region to decision-makers and influencers around the world. We support our public and private partners in their efforts to recruit new business and talent to the sixteen counties that make up our region. We do it by facilitating and protecting a regional brand, by identifying and helping address challenges to economic development, and by facilitating cooperation between and among our partners.

Given that there are many other public and private entities that market the region, why is CRP relevant?

CRP is the only organization that brings together private and public interests across 16 counties in North Carolina and South Carolina to position the region. We are a non-profit organization dedicated solely to the growth and vitality of Charlotte USA. We help our partners leverage a variety of tools to help them achieve their economic development. We also provide a forum for our partners to address potential conflicts and help break down barriers that may arise from municipal and geographic boundaries. In that respect, CRP has a unique role to play.

How do you see CRP's relationship with its partners evolving under your leadership?

Our public and private investors are critical to our success. Half of our revenue comes from public sources, and half from private sources. Our partners include large and small corporations, professional firms and media groups, the sixteen counties we represent and the North Carolina and South Carolina departments of commerce. Our Board of Directors represents an extensive array of stakeholders, including top executives representing the full diversity of business and industry within the Charlotte region, highly respected public officials, and leadership from our various colleges, universities and technical institutions. My job is to keep our partners fully engaged in making Charlotte USA globally competitive.

What do you perceive as the strengths of the region?

Charlotte and its surrounding region is full of potential. The best days of the region are ahead of it. Pittsburgh and St. Louis, two cities that I worked for prior to coming to Charlotte, were leading industrial economies 100 years ago. In the new economic age we live in, those two cities are working hard to reinvent themselves and position themselves for this century. Charlotte, on the other hand, is a city very much of this time and the century ahead. It is a city oriented toward the future, and its core strength is how aggressive the community is about improving itself and its standing and perception in the country and the world.

What challenges do you face marketing the region?

The two paramount challenges we face are "lack of product" and workforce development. By "lack of product," I mean site locations for businesses that need ready-to-go shell buildings with supporting infrastructure. Site location product has to be largely in place to attract businesses. Saying that you will build it after the fact of relocation doesn't cut it. Companies deciding between different markets rarely take that risk. They make the decision to move based on the existing product that is currently offered. The second challenge is workforce development: Our region needs to continue to address skill and literacy levels to attract knowledge-based companies.

What initiatives does CRP have underway to address these challenges?

We are putting together a "product development forum" that will happen this spring. It's the first of its kind that we are aware of. We will facilitate discussion and workshops on developing new site locations to attract business into the region, and talk about the best way to manage associated risks with forward funding and other financing options. We want this region to lead the way in having great product to offer businesses. We are also initiating an effort to deepen and broaden our strategic thinking on regional economic development issues. We want to make sure that our regional planning is current, comprehensive and relevant. We want to bring our stakeholders together to develop creative solutions. ⏻

Q&A with Tony Pressley

By Mark Peres

May 2005

Tony Pressley is president and CEO of MECA properties, a family-owned commercial and residential real estate company committed to revitalization of Charlotte's earliest urban communities and business corridors, including Historic South End. In 2001, he was named Charlotte Regional Realtor Association's (CRRA) Realtor of the Year, given the Public Relations Society of America/Charlotte Chapter Pegasus Award, and was named one of the top 15 entrepreneurs of the past 15 years by The Charlotte Business Journal. *Tony also received the 2000 Charlotte Chamber Entrepreneur Award, and the 1995 Realtor of the Year by the Charlotte Region Commercial Board of Realtors.*

Tell us about the history of Historic South End as we know it today.

While the neighborhood was established as a neighborhood in 1852 when the railroad arrived from the south, modern day history began in the early '90s. The City, recognizing that the original business corridors were suffering from disinvestment and becoming blighted, issued bonds to make improvements in hopes of jump-starting redevelopment. South Blvd. was the first such corridor to benefit, and the City invited a group of neighborhood "stakeholders" to participate in planning and prioritizing the improvements. As a result, a public-private partnership was born that continues today. The original stakeholder group went on to become an organized committee, then a non-profit and today is a special tax district raising some $300,000+ a year to fund ongoing neighborhood improvements and initiatives, like the recent Art and Soul Festival, among many other things.

How would you describe the character of Historic South End?

Historic South End has emerged as a Design District serving the region, and it is well on its way to distinguishing Charlotte as an emerging Design City of America. South End today has, at last count, 228 design firms (out of 450-500 businesses or so total) located in the District. While it's fascinating to some that a design district has emerged, the neighborhood has always had a strong tradition of innovation, creativity and design. What is happening today is merely a continuation of a legacy that started with D.A. Tompkins, E.D. Latta, Stewart Cramer, and other turn-of-the-last-century pioneers who I am sure are smiling favorably upon us.

What are the guiding principles of development in South End?

Everyone is welcome. Including Lowe's. However, anyone new to the area should take stock of what the area is all about and adapt to the environment. South End is urban. It has an Industrial/Manufacturing feel even to this day, and there is no place for the typical suburban model that some have tried and failed to impose on the community. The community is about density (since our available land mass is small), mixed-use, and as stated earlier, Innovation, Creativity and Design. Those that come into South End should strive to add value and can best achieve that by becoming engaged before putting the sticks and bricks on the ground or attempting to adaptively reuse one of the existing buildings.

How would you assess the district's relationship with Charlotte Center City Partners?

It's POSITIVE. We have been through a tough 2+ year transition period with staff turnover, but we are excited about Michael Smith being named to replace Tim Newman at Center City Partners. The decision to merge made good financial sense, it will help our neighborhood become stronger, and the sooner we get the entire Urban Center to come together with one voice, the better Charlotte will be able to compete with other Urban Centers. That is not to say we have to lose the South End "brand," or that any other Urban Neighborhood has to relinquish its character. There are many examples of how distinct neighborhoods have come together in other great cities.

What is the future of South End?

Great neighborhoods have to have a real economy, providing real jobs and real wages that create demand for housing, then services. We are playing out this model of development and feel truly blessed to have developed such a large following among the greater Design Industry. That industry is huge and even with all our success to date, we have not begun to scratch the surface as to what can be. It's for that reason we will continue to target every such opportunity. At the same time, we desire an improved quality of life and not just economic success. It's for that reason we will continue to embrace the arts, especially the emerging arts. Of course, the Trolley has had a tremendous positive impact on the neighborhood, and beginning in 2007 we will have Light Rail service. One challenge will be to manage the change, since, as I have said for some time, we can still screw this thing up. ⏻

Real Love

By Karen Martin, Charlotte ViewPoint Columnist

April 2006

Real estate. It has become a springtime ritual with me. There's something about the trees budding with promise, the warming winds breezing with possibility, the overall sense of rebirth and renewal.

When I was younger, it was boys. My mother says she always pitied the guy I was dating once springtime rolled around; she knew he would soon be going out like a lamb.

Now that I'm older, forget Match.com – my flirtations are with Realtor.com.

I've heard all the talk about the real estate "bubble," and how real estate investments can be risky these days. I can't help but feel, however, that finding the right piece of property is a lot like finding a good relationship: it may take some work, but it's well worth it.

Over the past 11 years I have owned five properties in the Charlotte area – in Dilworth, Myers Park, Elizabeth, NoDa and now Davidson – and, even with the tiniest capital gains due to timing – have made a tidy profit on each. It works out nicely for someone like me, who doesn't have the trust fund or the paycheck to be a big-time player in big-return investments.

My friends are doing just as well, if not better. Maria owns a rental property in Dilworth that she bought in 1991 for $80,000. Even with no significant improvements, that house today is worth $175,000. Joan bought her NoDa home – "on the cusp of the 'hood," she chuckles – four years ago for $80,000. "Now," she says of the houses on her street, "you can't get one for less than $250,000."

I love sharing the "how we met" story of my current home near the Davidson village green. Four years ago, my groom-to-be and I were weeks away from marrying when a real estate agent walked me through a bungalow on a different street. It was in a sad state of repair, with holes in the plywood flooring and an exterior staircase to the second floor. My groom decided the renovation would be too much for us at that time, so we instead bought a house in Elizabeth that already had been refurbished.

A year later, wearied by my husband's daily commute to Statesville, I drove by that house. The owners had completely updated it, bringing it back to life. That afternoon I accessed the Mecklenburg County tax records to find the owners' names and address. I sent them a note: if you ever want to sell your house, here's my phone number. Call me.

The phone rang the next afternoon. "We love this neighborhood, we love this house, and we're not moving," the woman said, "but there's a house nearby that you might want to check out." The owner hadn't lived there in four years, and now wanted to sell. It hadn't yet gone on the market.

We dropped by that nearby house, met the owner and within a week had a handshake agreement.

Prior to move-in, we gave our "new" pre-WWI bungalow a warm dose of TLC, entirely renovating and repainting, and replacing the mechanicals. (We later added a master suite plus bonus room, for a total investment of $157 per square foot. Our neighbors just sold their similar-sized home for about $190 per square foot, so assuming we could sell our place tomorrow for, let's say, only $180 per square foot, we're still looking at a healthy profit.)

Of course, affection has nothing to do with money. If we were to cash out and move, we would no longer be two blocks from our favorite pizza place, the public library and a coffee shop. We wouldn't be four blocks from the elementary school and a block from the middle school. We'd miss the way our plaster walls undulate. We'd miss our neighbors, who love their old houses as much as we do.

The real estate "bubble" may be about to burst elsewhere, but I feel confident about the viability of the Charlotte area's close-in neighborhoods. So good, in fact, that I'm looking at a potential rental property in what may be the next hot area. It needs a good deal of attention and hands-on quality time, but what happy relationship doesn't? ⏻

Q&A WITH BRUCE LAROWE

BY MARK PERES

MARCH 2006

Bruce LaRowe has served as the Executive Director of the Children's Theatre of Charlotte (CTC) since 1993. Previously, he served two years as Director of Development with Belmont Abbey College and eight years as Associate Director of the Arts & Science Council of Charlotte-Mecklenburg. As Executive Director of CTC, Bruce oversees all aspects of Theatre operations and programming. This season, in collaboration with the Charlotte-Mecklenburg Public Library, the Theatre opened its new home at ImaginOn: The Joe & Joan Martin Center – a $40 million facility that is among the most unique of its kind in the world. Bruce holds a B.A. in History from Millikin University in Decatur, IL, and a M.A. in Community Arts Management from Sangamon State University in Springfield, IL. He was a 2003-04 fellow in the Charlotte Region Chapter of the American Leadership Forum, an organization dedicated to strengthening established leaders in order to serve the public good.

Children's Theatre of Charlotte stands out as unique among professional theaters. How is it different?

Most children's theatres across the country tend to focus on one or two areas such as mounting productions or conducting classes or touring productions. The Children's Theatre is unique in that we are a "full service" theatre for youth, we have an active education program in schools and in the community, we mount a season of plays in ImaginOn, and we tour shows across the Southeast. The Children's Theatre is a professional theatre employing professional actors, technicians, and educators and serves audiences age 3-18.

The scope of the Theatre places it in the top five children's theatres nationally in terms of budget and audience served. Our current budget is $3.6 million comprising a full-time staff of 35 and a part-time staff of 25. This year we will serve over 300,000 young people and their families at our home in ImaginOn, in schools, at locations throughout the community, and across the southeast.

The Theatre has had quite a year. How would you assess the relocation to ImaginOn and the response to the current season?

The response to our programs has been outstanding. We are setting records in terms of ticket sales and class registrations. *The Lion, The Witch and The Wardrobe* broke all records for both attendance and ticket revenue. I think the fact of being downtown in a new location has attracted a great deal of interest. First-time visitors sample our programs and come back for additional offerings. I also know that we have benefited from visitors coming to the youth library spaces in ImaginOn as the Library has benefited from visitors to the Children's Theatre.

Tell us more about your community outreach and education.

I think most people would be surprised to know that we provide programs in every grade, K-12, of Charlotte-Mecklenburg Schools as well as many private schools. This year alone we will take programs to, or have classes visit us, from 110 of the 150 CMS school sites. These programs are all curriculum-based, developed in partnership with educators, and focused on the North Carolina Standard Course of Study.

One of our less-visible programs to the public is our Drama for Healthy Living. In partnership with CMS, we have created programs for teenage students which focus on the serious issues of dating violence and substance and alcohol abuse. To address dating violence, we have partnered with the Shelter for Battered Women of the United Family Services (as a part of the CMS Personal Health Issues Curriculum) to present both a play and role playing workshops in health classes for all CMS ninth grade students. The alcohol abuse program is focused on eighth grade students. The goal of the Drama for Healthy Living program is to help teenagers identify the warning signs of dangerous behavior and to provide them with the tools to make positive healthy choices. Drama is a unique means to convey and explore these messages.

Our Community Involvement Program provides opportunities for people who would otherwise not be able to afford to participate in Theatre programs. We conduct education programs in community sites, offer scholarships for students to participate in classes, and offer subsidized tickets for students and families to attend performances. The Arts and Science Council has called this a model program, and its scope and impact is unique among children's theaters in the country.

What is your budget and where is the money coming from? How would you assess your financial status?

Of our $3.6 million budget, 50% is earned income representing ticket sales, class tuition, touring fees and investment income. The remaining 50% of the budget is contributed income. It consists of 20% through the Arts and Science Council and ArtsTeach, 25% contributed from individuals, corporations and fundraising events and 5% government. Thanks, in part, to a committed volunteer Board, we are in a strong financial position, having completed 24 consecutive years without a deficit.

The city is moving away from subsidizing the operating expenses of arts organizations. How are arts organizations in Charlotte adjusting?

Arts organizations are increasingly required to generate more of their own revenue. I think the greatest growth opportunity is in contributions from individuals. Corporations have been very generous, but the needs of the cultural groups are outpacing the growth of corporate giving. I believe that is a national trend. As funding patterns evolve, not all organizations will be able to adjust. Those that have built strong relationships with their constituents will thrive, and for others it will be a very challenging environment.

Tell us about next year. What's on the horizon?

Next year will be very exciting for the Theatre with our new lineup of plays, classes and programs. In addition to our own work, we will continue to expand our shared programs with the Public Library in ImaginOn. There is great opportunity for shared programs around the common theme of storytelling – written stories of the Library and spoken stories of the Theatre. ⏻

The self one conceives

      Is an empirical self

            Or not a priori

Q&A WITH MARCIE KELSO
BY MARK PERES

JUNE 2004

Marcie Kelso has served as Executive Director of The Light Factory – Center for Photography and Film since July 2002. The Light Factory is known nationally as a leading center for its exhibitions and educational programs centered on photography and film. Marcie came to the Charlotte region in February of 1996 from the Virginia Film Office to begin the Film Division of the Charlotte Regional Partnership. Under Marcie's stewardship, the Film Division recruited over 21 full-length productions and numerous commercials to the area, among them Shallow Hal, The Patriot, and Having Our Say. Marcie's community involvement in Charlotte has included serving on the board of The Light Factory, the Foundation for the Carolinas Impact Fund, and the Women's Cabinet of the Charlotte Jewish Federation. She is a graduate of the College of William & Mary in Williamsburg, Virginia, with degrees in both Government and Theatre & Speech.

What is the mission of The Light Factory?

We help promote the power of photography and film, the most influential medium in society. The Light Factory helps people experience the art of imagery, and we help empower them to create images of their own. Thousands of people visit The Light Factory each year to view our exhibitions, take classes, hear lectures and see films. We offer year-round classes in photography and filmmaking. Our outreach programs in the Charlotte community serve students of all ages and backgrounds. The Light Factory is the only non-profit 501-C3 center for photography and film in North Carolina, South Carolina and Virginia.

Who is your audience? Whom do you serve?

We serve a very broad audience. Everyone relates to TV, movies, photographs and images. The Light Factory is a contemporary art space where the artists we showcase are alive and commenting. We served over 60,000 people last year, and demographically they were across the board.

Tell us about your new exhibits. What should we know?

Our current exhibit is "Fabricated Harmony," which features American artist Pat Ward Williams and South African artist Sue Williamson. We commissioned new work from both of them in which they explore racial integration in the United States and South Africa. "The Freedom Box" exhibit is the result of our international outreach exchange program. The box is a symbolic representation of a slave who mailed himself to freedom in the late 1800's. Students from local CMS high schools joined students from several high schools in South Africa to create the exhibit. In March, we're launching a new exhibit called "Threshold of India," which is the result of artist Martha Strawn's 20-year visual ecology project. The exhibition includes photography and live threshold painting, which is an ancient Indian tradition in which women create rice flour designs on the ground outside the doors of homes. The exhibit celebrates the threshold practice and its place in the history of Hindu culture.

Tell us more about your education and outreach programs.

We offer classes in photography, darkroom film exposure, screenwriting and filmmaking. We offer our students hands-on experience with working professionals. We want to provide educational programs that promote media literacy. Our outreach programs touch the lives of thousands of students in the community, serving students from kindergarten to high school. One of our outreach programs, called 'My Family, My Stories' works with students who speak English as a second language. The students take photographs of their families, and then they write stories in English that accompany the images. That's one example of how we work to help people become more literate in an increasingly visual world.

What are your thoughts on the film and digital divide?

The divide has been breached. Although we still teach film-based photography and celebrate film as an art, the debate is over. In the last couple of years, commercial photography has become entirely digital. Art forms change with technology. At the turn of the 20th century, photography changed from platinum palladium based film to silver based film. At the turn of this century, photography has changed from film to digital. With each change, new possibilities present themselves.

What does The Light Factory do well? What do you want it to do better?

We're good at helping make the eye and mind work together. We're 30 years old, and over the last three years we've worked hard to become a more professionally managed organization. We're unique in our region, and we want to reach out more to all corners of the community. We welcome volunteers who would like to help us further our mission. ⏻

CMS: The Road Ahead

By Kit Cramer, Group Vice President, Charlotte Chamber of Commerce
Vice Chair, Charlotte-Mecklenburg Board of Education

November 2005

Public education is central to our democracy. It is the foundation upon which we build quality of life and our economic health. It requires the active participation of citizens. In Charlotte, we need more than participation. We need support.

It has been tough serving on the school board in the last year. We've faced a divided community over pupil assignment issues, competing interests over facility needs and concerns about discipline in our schools, all with a school board that is sometimes as visibly divided as is the community.

Despite differences in how things should be done, the School Board has sought to address these concerns in a variety of ways: 1) with a comprehensive review of student assignment, 2) by proposing $427 million in bonds to meet both growth and renovation needs, and 3) by asking Interim Superintendent Frances Haithcock to develop a comprehensive program to improve discipline, student behavior and safety.

We've also asked for greater transparency in the communications from the district and have called on state leaders for help with obtaining more qualified teachers and principals in an effort to boost student performance.

Amidst all the ancillary issues, we've been focused on student achievement. Our End of Grade test scores showed the percent of students at or above grade level in elementary reading is 86%, up one point and at 90% for math, down two points. Seven elementary schools had more than 10-point gains this year.

In middle schools, the percentage of students at or above grade level in reading is 82%, up two points. For math, the score remained steady at 84%.

The composite score for End of Course tests in the high schools is up three points for a total of 66%. While a lot of progress still needs to be made in our high schools, we're encouraged that the trend line is positive. A new initiative focused on high school performance has many exciting components.

While we're all anxious for even more improvement in all of our schools, the big picture view is that the achievement gap has narrowed by over 36 points since 1996! There aren't many districts of our size and composition that can make the same statement, and we salute the educators who have bucked the trend and made it happen.

As for the challenges from the last year, we've produced a pupil assignment plan that is simpler and easier to navigate, requiring fewer buses and giving all areas of the county access to popular magnet programs. Planning continues on the development of a military school and other unique programs – especially at the high school level – that we hope will capture the imagination of students and parents and improve our results.

At the first meeting in August, the Board heard a presentation on the comprehensive approach CMS will take to improving student behavior, discipline and safety. Dr. Haithcock worked with her staff to develop a project charter that assigns milestone dates, measures and responsibility for improving the learning environment of our schools. She has also invited representatives from all the public safety entities to join in on the implementation of the plan.

On November 8th voters will determine the outcome of the $427 million dollar bond referendum. The dollars devoted to growth and renovations within the request are proportional to the needs that have been outlined in the long-range facilities master plan.

As soon as the new district members of the school board are installed, we'll launch into a formal superintendent search. Our plan is to take our thoughts on what we're seeking to the public in a series of meetings in December.

We'll also be bringing the community a statement of our core beliefs and commitments to our schools, along with our strategic approach to improving student achievement. We'll be asking everyone to sign on in a show of support for public education.

The work of the school system can be contentious, demanding and frustrating. But it is also incredibly important… important to our children's future, important to the health and vitality of our economy and quality of life, important for Charlotte's continued success. Our community has a long, rich tradition of supporting public schools. We need to redouble that effort. ⏻

The Edge is Opportunity

By Ray "Rip" Farris III, Managing Member, Tuscan Development

February 2005

Dynamic and healthy cities resonate with diverse economic layers and cultures. Charlotte must protect and support diversity. The city must not only foster historical ethnic diversity, but diversity in its availability of lower-priced housing options for our multi-layered society.

Defining housing stands as a critical element to achieving these objectives.

Center City Charlotte has experienced tremendous change over the past twelve years. There is an emerging need to develop a coherent urban strategy that offsets the rising land price and the typical impediments to lower-and moderate-priced housing. Nationally, our region is second to Las Vegas in terms of growth over the past twelve years. And that growth pattern projected out twenty years, points to a rise in our metropolitan statistical area from the current 1.3 million to 4+ million residents. That is staggering growth.

Now is the time to face difficult and too often unpopular urban development policy choices.

With more than $5 billion invested in the redevelopment of the Center City, land prices have risen to the extent that the average price per square foot for residential exceeds $32, a cost that prevents moderately priced housing opportunities. These increased land values require increased density, public/private cooperation and creative development. Land prices in the Center City are much higher in part due to UMUD zoning – and its maximized density options. Perception among certain UMUD landowners suggests that the most probable and best use of land is commercial, in part because of perceived higher economic returns. These land economic conditions significantly reduce the possibility of housing prices affordable to those who earn near our median income level of $43,000 per year.

Most of the present housing offerings cater to the "dominant" rather than the "diverse." Typically we portray the dominant – the single-family detached suburban house – as the cultural norm, the ideal and standard. Even the term for the physical structure of the dwelling – the "single family" home – presumes a certain elevated social structure. We cannot allow our current social trends and housing patterns to fail the need for many forms of housing.

The troubling reality here is the gap of in-town housing affordability. Many poor single parents cannot live near their workplaces; some spend more than two hours daily commuting between home, work and day care, thus leaving little time to spend with their children. Day care and public transportation are often unavailable when the working poor and lower middle class work outside the nine-to-five workday hours.

However, surrounding the Center City are edge conditions that fall between our established neighborhoods. These areas offer the most opportunity for housing development because of reduced land cost. These edge conditions present a prime opportunity to explore public and private collaboration utilizing transit-oriented development concepts, joint-venture development models and urban development concepts not typical in Charlotte.

It is into these edge neighborhoods that people with the interest, but perhaps not the budget, to live in-town might be attracted. These edge areas are generally less-defined in physical terms, i.e., density or architectural character, and they generally have a substantial number of vacant parcels and buildings. Edge neighborhoods present unfettered options to explore planning, urban design, open space and architectural typologies. But they also present challenges, especially in terms of integration and gentrification. Our neighborhoods reach back to the late 1700s and memory remains quite powerful. We need to do a better job acknowledging our past layers.

Urban design, efficient architecture, public and private partnerships and planning policy can assist in the needed offset for land price and zoning challenges. The private sector provides knowledge, efficiency (cost and speed) and entrepreneurial skill, as well as freedom from legal restrictions that tend to bind the public sector (equity can be more important to the public sector). The public sector provides formal powers (eminent domain, regulatory approval, zoning and informal powers, infrastructure, cash-subsidies in the form of tax subsidies, grants and other non-cash assets).

Perhaps in the next few years, we can see an emergence of change in the way we perceive and approach these forgotten and often underutilized blocks of city fabric. Indeed, these neighborhoods are gifts to help us inform and diversify the city. ⏻

Charlotte Squawks

Center City Ambassadors

Hayes George Gallery

Jump'n Joe's Java Joint

JWU International Film Series

Reading the Obits

By Mark Peres, Charlotte ViewPoint Editor

December 2004

I read the paper today and stopped on the obituaries. It's not something I normally do. The temperature is dropping. Leaves are falling. Bare branches are showing. Winter can catch you in its chill, as faces of the dead can do off a page.

Here and there are short little biographies, entire lives condensed to a paragraph or two. Marriages and careers, awards and recognitions, all reduced to an economic report, making sure to mention the names of the predeceased and the surviving, and where to send the flowers. Each obituary a headstone, the headstones together a cemetery, the cemetery as impermanent as newsprint, as tomorrow's run is prepared.

We see the photographs. Young and old. Black and white. Women and men. Death is democratic, embracing the whole of our body politic, leaving no one behind. Who chooses the last image? The last image that says more in a final glance than any word? The last image reminding us of our own inevitable fate.

So what to do with this life?

It's the stuff of shaman and rabbis, of high priests and street-corner prophets. It's the stuff of kings and midwives, of architects and existentialists. It is, ultimately, the stuff of art, of objects and time, and the creative destruction of the seasons.

Do all you can with what you have in this time and place. So we join the Chamber, we love our children, and we balance the books. Live for the moment. Tomorrow is not guaranteed. So we buy the new car, we write our novel, and we cross state lines. If we do it right, by some measure, we get special mention in the paper, with a testimonial from a long-standing friend.

My dad died five years ago. He was 82. He traveled the world and spoke several languages. He was an immigrant and salesman of this and that. He laughed and cried and struggled. He was married for 45 years and raised five children. He could weave stories about Zionism, the Brazilian rainforest, and the rise and fall of the Roman empire. I don't remember reading his obituary, and I'm not sure I would find any reflection of him in one if I had.

I see my daughter and her friends in grade school. They wheel backpacks that are out-of-scale and wear uniforms of blue and white. A century of wonder and electrons, of space travel and terror, is in front of them. My daughter is so present in the moment. I see photos of her at her birth, and ask where the days have gone.

I look in the mirror and see a mish-mosh of genetic code, and the creative destruction of the seasons. So what to do with this life? What legacy will it be? Will it be a disconnect or some walk toward truth? Will it be a missed opportunity or will a light shine from within?

I live in this town of finance and clean streets. Money flows, civility reigns and gardens are kept up. The town is forward thinking, optimistic and temperate in all things. As middle as middle can be, with a gleam and a shine, and history as important as yesterday's newsprint. There is, in it, a yearning to matter. To make something of today at yesterday's expense, to impart convention as a beauty, the norm as an ideal.

It is tempting to personify the city, to reduce her to a paragraph or two, to see in her a life a future of awards and recognition. At the end of days, what will her obituary say? She earned a handsome living and she went to church. Will it say much else? Will it say she did all she could do with what she had in her time and place? Will it say she moved toward the light of art, exploring objects and time?

The opportunity as citizens is in choosing our last image. ⏻

Knight

Middl

McMi

Galler

Wacho

Galler

McGlohon
Theatre

Duke Power
Theatre

nances

Dance

Music

Theat

Q&A WITH TOM GABBARD

BY MARK PERES

AUGUST 2005

Tom has been President of the North Carolina Blumenthal Performing Arts Center for two years. He directs a full-time staff of 90 who manage four theaters, studios, classrooms and offices for 14 resident companies. The Center is one of the leading presenters of the performing arts in the Southeast, and typically ranks in the top 10 performing arts centers in North America. He has directed art centers in Malibu, Denver and Green Bay. Tom is a member of the Board of Governors of the League of American Theatres and Producers and is a voter for Broadway's Tony Awards. He is active in the commercial theater as a co-producer/investor in Broadway productions, national tours and London West End, including winning a Tony Award recently as a co-producer of Monty Python's Spamalot.

What is the role and charge of the North Carolina Blumenthal Performing Arts Center?

The Center focuses on three primary tasks. First, we are managers of the community's key performing arts facilities. Second, we are presenters who bring to Charlotte the best in the performing arts by filling niches in programming that are not already covered by local groups like the Symphony, Opera and Dance Theatre. Third, we're educators who work with schools and adults to use the arts to improve learning and provide cultural enrichment.

Charlotte is a dynamic city with changing demographics. What challenge and opportunity does that present to you?

We're blessed by a growing population and audience to serve. However, it's a challenge to keep up with what the community needs from us. The region is becoming ethnically more diverse. There's also been a large influx of young professionals. We must continuously look for ways to assure that our programs and services are relevant. With so many newcomers, we also have an important role in helping to create a sense of community. It's not easy to "get connected" in a new city. Sharing a performance with neighbors and business associates can be immensely helpful to feeling part of this community.

What is the relationship between the NCBPAC and the Arts & Science Council? How would you assess the relationship?
The Center's relationship with the ASC has not always been good. Some have argued that we should break off from the ASC since they feel we'd be more successful with our fund raising if we were independent. Thanks to the leadership of Lee Keesler, the new CEO of the ASC, we now work very well together. We get a relatively small amount of money from the ASC, barely 1% of our budget. There's a misconception that the ASC's funding supplies all the needs of arts groups rather just one small piece. Maybe our fund raising would be better on our own, however, it's important to consider the big picture and the good the ASC does for the entire cultural scene of which we are a part.

Some believe that more basic city services should have priority for tax dollars over the proposed new arts and cultural facilities. What are your thoughts?
We need reasonable support of both to create a thriving city that people want to live and work in. The City has a good track record of partnership with the community to support arts and culture, and I hope that continues. However, our sense of civic pride shouldn't lead us to think our efforts have been exceptional. I'd say they are about average for a growing city of this size. Charlotte's thriving Center City is due to many things, but building and operating the Blumenthal clearly was one part of turning it around. When you consider Wachovia's plan to either build a tower of $90 million without arts facilities, or a mixed-use development of $300 million by adding the arts facilities, you can see how the arts encourage both a strong business climate and beneficial quality of life.

How would you describe the City's approach to art? How would you like to see it evolve?
The arts are a little more "buttoned-up" in Charlotte, but I also see a strong interest in loosening up. As compared with other cities I've worked in, support for the arts is more about civic good than passion for the art itself. I don't hear from people as often, pro or con, about the artistic elements of what we put on our stages. Audiences here are a little more "brand conscious." People like to see things that have been successful elsewhere or have won awards. I'd love to see more support for new work and things that are created locally. However, for that to happen, we need to instill more pride in new and locally created work, and have tolerance that it may not be perfect yet. I think we can make progress if we keep enriching the public's understanding with more background information about what they're seeing. Lastly, I'm thrilled to see a resurgence of interest in funkier, older facilities like Spirit Square that for awhile were out of favor as new buildings popped up. Diversity of spaces is healthy for us. ⏻

MARCH 2006

It's an exciting time to live in my native hometown of Charlotte, and the excitement is everywhere. Look around, and you'll see 360 degrees of successes in the measures that make a city livable. Growth and development (hopefully managed) bring vertical reality to progress. Take the pulse of the city in conversations and notice the feeling of optimism. It's more than our perpetual spirit of boosterism – this city has palpable momentum. Charlotte is becoming more inviting and more desirable.

I've been thinking about how all this came to be, and about what remains to be done. The pride that I have in our recent string of successes, entertainment facilities, a newly acquired tournament, and successful non-profit fund drives is tempered by the awareness of human services needs, the lack of affordable housing, and an education system that screams for help on all levels. These community problems are being addressed on many fronts, and while there are no easy solutions, it's encouraging that these issues have the attention of our decision-makers. We live in a community that values progress, which we measure not only in glass and steel, but also in enhanced lives.

What kind of leadership does it take to tackle weighty issues in the here and now, and also to think in the future tense? What skills are required for mastery of the complex dynamic of serving the public? What do leaders need to know? The first step in leadership development can be found in Socrates' quote, "Know thyself." So, it makes sense that one of the global leadership universals is personal literacy – understanding and valuing yourself. It's a logical step from self-awareness to then understanding others. Personally literate leaders will move our community forward with aggressive insight, confident humility, authentic flexibility, reflective decisiveness and realistic optimism.

Other twenty-first century leadership competencies include social literacy – engaging and challenging people, and cultural literacy – valuing and leveraging cultural differences. Cultural literacy is critical in our diverse society and our global environment. Leaders who master these competencies are more effective at being exemplary leaders. According to Kouzes and Posner, leaders who are exemplary share these practices. They model the way, inspire a shared vision, challenge the process, enable others to act, and encourage the heart.

I think the practice most needed is being able to inspire a shared vision. Leaders who passionately believe that they can make a difference envision the future, creating an ideal and unique image of what the organization/business/city can become. Through their magnetism and quiet persuasion, they enlist others in their dreams. They breathe life into their visions and get people to see exciting possibilities for the future. People want to follow them. Charlotte is indebted to generations of leaders who were able to successfully communicate their vision and inspire others to follow. I can imagine years of conversations where our tireless volunteer community leaders dreamed and hoped about what Charlotte could become if only…

Then, they worked to fill that void with ballot initiatives, with public-private partnerships, with bond campaigns, with fundraising campaigns, with numerous civic efforts designed to achieve the desired ends. I am thankful that in 2006, our leadership at the decision-making level is more diverse. This inclusiveness taps the full potential of the community and the richness of our ideas.

In the past several years our community experienced a shift in leadership, when several established leaders moved off the stage. These changes raised the question, "Is there a leadership gap?" We quickly saw the void being filled by new voices with fresh ideas and new energy. My hope is that these leaders will continue the commitment to progress and will follow their passions to effecting change in a positive way.

Leadership guru Max DePree said, "Perhaps a way to think about the difference between sight and vision is this: We can teach ourselves to see things the way they are. Only with vision can we begin to see things the way they can be." To our benefit, Charlotte has been fortunate to have leaders who saw things the way they could be. And, leaders who adhere to a quote that was overheard at the recent "Foursight" forum: "The only thing worse than vision without action is action without vision." These are words to lead by. ⏻

Q & A with Christie Taylor
BY JENNIFER GARNER

MAY 2006

Christie Taylor is the Managing Partner of Hodges Taylor Gallery on North Tryon Street. She has managed the business with her partner, Dot Hodges, for over 25 years. Prior to opening Hodges Taylor, Christie managed Art Gallery Originals in Winston-Salem and McNeal Gallery in Charlotte. Christie has served on several community boards, including The Junior League of Charlotte, where she chaired the Homeless Awareness Committee, Habitat for Humanity, serving as the volunteer public relations coordinator for Habitat for Humanity's Miracle on 34th Street, and was instrumental in the organization of the Visual Arts Coalition: a visual arts political action committee to serve as a united voice for artists in the community. She is a former president of The Light Factory, and is currently chairman of Chamber Music at St. Peter's Episcopal Church. Christie received a degree in art from Queens College.

Why does art matter in Charlotte?

Goodness, that's like asking "Why do we need air!" Let me just sum up my response in this quote by Henry Miller: "Art teaches nothing, except the significance of life."

How did an art major end up owning a gallery?

I think a lot of gallery owners had dreams about becoming artists. When I was eight years old, my drawing, A Day at the Circus, was awarded a blue ribbon. My parents framed it and hung it in our home! The personal satisfaction of being acknowledged for my own creative expression; to see the pleasure and delight my image brought to others has made a lifelong impression on me. I certainly had found my passion. I continued my interest in art throughout my academic career. When I graduated from Queens, I realized that I had developed a stronger passion to promote the contribution of artists to our lives and to assist others in discovering themselves through art. At the time, honestly, it was a better fit for me rather than pursuing a career as a painter. I didn't have enough life experience to have something to "say" visually. The choice I made continues to enrich my life daily.

Who inspired/influenced you?

My parents. As I mentioned, framing my drawing was a statement of faith in me as an artist. They also played a role in encouraging my entrepreneurial spirit. At an early age, I observed the importance of identifying a mission that matters in life, the willingness to take responsibility and the thrill of the challenge to accomplish goals. My mother led by example. She taught me the importance of volunteerism as I watched her run the Garden Club Council and chair the first Beautification/Don't Litter campaign in Winston-Salem. I took on her commitment, much to the dismay of my friends, as I would stop the car and make them pick up gum wrappers that they mistakenly had thrown out the car window. It is a little known fact, but my father was the visionary behind the state highway flower program, right up there with Lady Bird Johnson! As he traveled for Wachovia, my mother would load the truck of his car with flower seeds and he would pull off the highway and scatter them along the road.

So, with their guidance and their gift of playfulness, I took on leadership roles in high school and college. I naturally gravitated towards "community" by serving as President of the Teen Council in Winston-Salem, a citywide organization to study teen issues and plan events. At Queens College, I served as President of the Student Union for two terms. We established "The Pit," a gathering place for students, and we coordinated all events on campus. This experience landed me my first experience in the art gallery business. If I knew how to book bands, play hostess, handle money, deal with the public and delight in watching others enjoy themselves, then I could manage artists and a gallery. Oh, and yes, I even took out the trash. Influences as for my artistic endeavors? Miss Walton, my third grade teacher, John Fox, my high school teacher, and Dr. George Shealy, head of the art department at Queens. They, too, all had faith in me as an artist. I am very grateful.

Why did you chose uptown as a location for your gallery?

The main street of a city is where you can find all walks of life. We believe that no one person is greater than another in the presence of a work of art. This philosophy puts us on Tryon Street where we can all learn to see, rather than know. What should Charlotte do to encourage and support artists? Be curious! I am on a personal crusade to launch a campaign about curiosity in Charlotte. We are a great town about recognizing the arts as good business, with lots of bricks and mortar to support its growth, but how do we get people to be curious about seeking out experiences that push beyond entertainment?

My business is about celebrating the self-expression in all of us. And, I believe self-expression begins with curiosity. As adults, (not to mention children staring at TV and computers all day) coupled with the pace of our lives, we are losing touch with our senses. Let's wake them up! So how about this as a campaign idea? What if we all wore buttons that stated what we had wanted to be when we grew up? Think about it. Walking down Tryon Street, you would pass strangers that had cowboy/cowgirl pinned to their suit. Think how differently we would relate to each other. Think how we would relate to ourselves. I truly believe IF we are willing to reconnect to the "curious child" in each of us, there would be more people in the seats at cultural events, more creative dialogue around the corporate table and even more kids staying in school. I know how fortunate I am that I have a career that encourages me to wear that ARTIST button that I put on at age eight. And, I feel very fortunate that I get to witness the curiosity in others in front of a work of art. So what would YOUR button say? ⏻

Gladiators battle

Hearts aflutter

A thrilling Valentine

MAGIC, MOMENTS & MEMORIES
BY TIM NEWMAN, PRESIDENT, CHARLOTTE CENTER CITY PARTNERS

APRIL 2004

So where does the Center City go from here? In the wake of Charlotte Center City Partners' first-ever public annual meeting and quarterly board meeting, there is much on the table at this point in our history. Despite a tough economy and the post-September 11th environment, we have over $500 million in new construction underway, highlighted by Johnson & Wales' new campus to debut this fall, our new arena that will open in 2005 featuring the Bobcats and Sting, and ImaginOn, the beautiful new children's learning center that will open next year. Now that these facilities are coming online and the economy is picking up, we have the opportunity to take the Center City to new levels in three areas: jobs, amenities and events.

On the jobs front, we are working closely with the Charlotte Chamber of Commerce and the Charlotte Regional Partnership on economic development prospects to grow the employment base in the Center City. We are seeking to bring companies here that have business ties with our current employers. The greater our employment base, the greater the likelihood of amenities and events coming to our neighborhood.

We continue to seek dining, shopping and other entertainment amenities to make the Center City a great place to live and play. At our board meeting on March 18th, Spectrum Properties gave an overview of redevelopment plans for the old Convention Center. Highlights include a multiscreen movie theater, roof-top dining and entertainment, and bold colors, lighting and signage. The new urban entertainment complex will make a wonderful attraction replacing a vacant eyesore. Final details on the project will be forthcoming in the next few weeks. Last week, at our annual meeting, International Downtown Association President Dave Feehan noted in his keynote address that the best downtowns are those that provide magic, moments and memories. Charlotte is right on track to create a vibrant and attractive Center City experience that will entertain, educate and inspire residents and visitors alike.

Events in the Center City continue to reach new heights. "Taste of the Nation" arrives in Charlotte on April 6th and 7th, "Avenue of the Arts" and "Taste of Charlotte" roll around May 1st and 2nd, and "Charlotte Shout" will be bigger and better this September with Master Chefs Martin Yan and Tyler Florence already confirmed for our Culinary Experience.

It's a great time to be in the Center City, and I appreciate the opportunity to share my thoughts with you. Did I mention that we may soon have a full-service drug store with night and weekend hours? I'll see you around the neighborhood. ⏻

Q&A with Clay Grubb

By Mark Peres

January 2006

Clay Grubb is President of Grubb Properties, a real estate company that developed The Ratcliffe and Latta Pavilion, and is currently developing Elizabeth Avenue and Morrison Place. He is a graduate of Tulane University with a double major in finance and economics. Clay received his law degree from the University of North Carolina at Chapel Hill. He is a seven-year member, past president and treasurer of the Charlotte Apartment Association (CAA) and is currently a member of the Young Presidents Organization, the Urban Land Institute and Queens University's Entrepreneurial Circle, where he previously served as a member of the Board of Trustees. Clay recently received the CAA 2005 Lex Marsh Award for industry leadership and outstanding individual membership.

Your company has positioned itself as an urban, infill, mixed-use developer. Why did you choose that market?
Several factors led us to this strategy. First, a growing realization that national firms coming into Charlotte could build a lot faster and cheaper than we could in the suburbs and around the I-485 interchanges. Second, our market trends analysis in the late '90s indicated strong and growing demand for mixed-use infill projects to combat sprawl and revitalize historic neighborhoods. And third, the reality that these kinds of projects are never cookie-cutter – they require local expertise, community relationships, and the blend of skills we've developed over four decades in the residential, retail and office markets. In this kind of market, we believe that we can add value and compete strongly with anyone.

What principles of development guide your work?
Our first principle is simply to create value – for our communities, our investors and ourselves. If that doesn't happen, nothing else will either. In addition, we don't get involved in anything we wouldn't want to own 10 years down the road. This leads us to projects that age well in prime locations, which means we'll have numerous exit opportunities along the way as well as a comfort level in holding the assets if we choose or need to do so. Other than that, we try to follow Wayne Gretsky's advice and "skate to where the puck is going to be, not to where it is." We've enjoyed our best results over the years when we've gotten out ahead of the curve, but whether we're working on a cutting-edge project or our core portfolio, a "whatever it takes" mentality is often the biggest factor in our success.

What development challenges and opportunities do inner-ring neighborhoods in Charlotte present?

The opportunities probably go without saying – enhancing and revitalizing the communities closest to the urban core, and even building bridges between those communities with the flow of private and public capital and resources. Mixed-use urban infill is not for the faint of heart, though – it is time-consuming, expensive and unpredictable. One of the lessons we learned with Latta Pavilion in Dilworth, which was coming to market right around 9/11, was to design more flexibility into a project in order to accommodate unexpected swings in the consumer and financial markets. Getting all the land under control is also critical – our Morrison project in SouthPark, for example, is much simpler than what we're doing along Elizabeth Avenue.

Many people believe that Charlotte is a town controlled and driven by developers. What's your response?

You could predict my response, of course, but I'd have to disagree. Good development shapes the image of a city and attracts the growth and vibrancy all of us who live here want to see. The city knows this, of course, and has an appreciation for the challenges inherent in infill mixed-use development. So do the banks, who have developed or influenced more of Charlotte's landscape than all the developers combined. The Ratcliffe is a prime example of Wachovia pushing against conventional wisdom in favor of an upscale landmark project that went on to sell out in six months and raise the bar for Center City residential development. In the end, we have an influx of employers, families, restaurants, shopping, sports and entertainment – as well as revitalization projects that have, or will, transform neighborhoods and lives across the city. The city knows what it wants and is helpful to developers who are aligned with that vision, but they certainly haven't forgotten how to say "no."

What projects by other developers are noteworthy to you?

Trademark, Avenue, The Vue…all of the Uptown condominium projects are impressive. They're really setting a tone for the future, as did The Ratcliffe and 400 North Church when they were developed. Not to mention the whole First Ward project, because it combines with the others to offer a spectrum of residential options within the city. This spectrum is important – I've said since 1999 that it wasn't possible to overbuild the Center City, but you can price people out of the market, and it's important not to do that. SouthPark Mall is incredibly noteworthy as well. Simon has reenvisioned retail in this market, transforming an aging mall into the strongest retail environment between Atlanta and Washington, D.C. We're all seeing retailers and restaurants in the area now that previously wouldn't have even considered locating in Charlotte. Simon's work there has been just a great boost to SouthPark and the city overall.

How is the Elizabeth Avenue project coming along?

Well, it's a great project for Grubb Properties and for Charlotte – but one that is very complex – so we're hopefully optimistic that the pieces will continue to fall in place. So far, our first spec building – 1523 Elizabeth Avenue – is almost fully leased and we've placed two high-visibility tenants – Carpe Diem restaurant and NOFO gift shop and café – into beautifully renovated existing spaces where they both report stronger-than-ever sales. We think they're strongly validating the appeal of this location for the right uses. This year is key, though – the city begins work along Elizabeth Avenue in preparation for widening the sidewalks and laying tracks for the streetcar line, and we'll start construction on the Whole Foods site at the corner of 4th Street, Hawthorne and Elizabeth. The last piece of that puzzle is relocating our tenant Burger King to make way for Whole Foods. Burger King has bought into the larger vision and the importance of Elizabeth Avenue to the city – it's just a matter of working out the details of the move.

What development issue needs greater attention?

As a city and as developers, we need to make sure we don't leave working people behind. Charlotte has a long history – sometimes good, sometimes not – of being a place where people from all walks of life mingled together throughout the city. Going forward, there are several key components to getting this right, in no particular order. One, we need to continue integrating affordable housing into Uptown development. Two, more public-private partnerships are needed to reinvigorate historic neighborhoods. The Piedmont Courts revitalization project alongside the proposed Kroc Center campus in Belmont is a great example of this in action…development bringing transportation, education, recreation, social services and not just jobs but networking opportunities to our most challenged communities. And third, we need to address any impact of displacing working-class families as neighborhoods undergo transformation – every citizen and every family has a stake in the future of this city, and each of us deserves a voice in creating the vision for that future. ⏻

CENTER CITY: THE CAROLINAS HOT SPOT
BY MICHAEL SMITH, PRESIDENT, CHARLOTTE CENTER CITY PARTNERS

AUGUST 2005

Take a stroll through today's Center City. It's a far cry from the after-five ghost town of the prior two decades. Today, the Center City is the hot spot of the Carolinas for nightlife and urban living. We are fulfilling the vision of the 2010 Vision Plan with great housing and entertainment options. We have reached a true tipping point as our workforce has grown to 65,000 workers and our residential population will grow to approximately 15,000 by 2008.

With the achievement of an active nightlife and wonderful restaurants, an explosive growth in residential and a strong and growing office population, we will face new challenges in planning, events management, parking, public safety, transportation and transit. Our latest challenge in support of our growth is the changing needs of public safety. We have achieved wonderful growth in the number of people who come to the Center City on weekend nights for entertainment. These numbers include arts patrons, young professionals enjoying our nightlife and a new phenomenon is teens who are using the streets for cruising and the sidewalks for socializing. Cruising and excessive crowds on the sidewalks limit access by first responders (police, fire and medic), reduces traffic flow on streets and sidewalks and thus can limit commerce.

To deal swiftly with this problem, Charlotte Center City Partners has formed a public safety task force that includes Police Chief Darrel Stephens, Mayor Pat McCrory, City Manager Pam Syfert, and members of our Board, including club and restaurant owners and business leaders.

The recommendations of this task force included an immediate increased police presence in the Center City on the weekend nights when crowds are at their peak. This swift action has made a major impact. The Chief is also creating an Entertainment District Unit that will include 10 officers assigned to the Entertainment district for weekends. They will be on bikes, on foot and in cars to intervene swiftly, to address changing crowd patterns and to be the constant presence on the street. Another recommendation is to change the traffic patterns along Tryon Street on Friday and Saturday nights to interrupt cruising. Many of these recommendations have already been implemented.

Other strategies of the Task Force are longer-term to keep Center City safe 24/7. At the top of that list is a call for more and better lighting on our streets and in parking lots. As we speak, teams with C-DOT are doing a complete inventory of lighting in the Center City, especially in our entertainment district around the Arena and the nightclubs and in the residential areas. They are evaluating the effectiveness of lights along streets and in parking lots and identifying places where more lighting is needed.

Center City Partners is creating an Ambassador Program. Initially, the Ambassadors will be deployed around the new Arena during the first wave of events. Our Ambassadors will be the friendly faces with the information visitors need. Eventually, our Ambassador program will expand to include other events and special occasions.

We are also working with parking lot operators to staff their property with attendants. We are asking them to actively cooperate with police to allow patrols through the lots. We are confident this plan is working and will continue to be effective.

We are primed for a wonderful decade of continued evolution for the Center City. Before the end of the year, the new Arena and ImaginOn will open. Within two years, more than 3,000 units of housing will come on line, more than half in high-rise condominiums. The EpiCentre opens on Trade Street with entertainment and more than 250,000 square feet of retail space. Wachovia has proposed to build a cultural arts, office and residential campus on South Tryon. We are competing for the NASCAR Hall of Fame. Ritz Carlton is coming in partnership with Bank of America. All of these milestones will create animation, economic expansion and new challenges.

We will continue to support this momentum and enhance our vibrant and safe Center City that is welcoming and accessible to all. We believe we have plans in place to do just that. ⏻

ARENA | PROJECT

PROJECT ADMINISTRATION	CITY OF CHARLOTTE ENGINEERING AND PROPI
PRIME ARCHITECT	ELLERBE BECKET, INC.
ASSOCIATE ARCHITECT	ODELL ASSOCIATES, INC.
ASSOCIATE ARCHITECT	FREELON
CIVIL AND LANDSCAPE	COLEJENEST & STONE
CONSTRUCTION MANAGER	

The Charlotte Arena and Uptown Development

By Barry Silberman, Executive Vice President, Charlotte Bobcats

September 2004

Now that the Arena is magnificently rising from the ground and starting to take its structural form, one might wonder: What other concerns does an arena manager have? One of the greatest potential opportunities resulting from the development of the Arena is in the realm of future development maximization for the City. Because of its advantageous location in Uptown, the arena is poised to be a magnet for all types of exciting residential, retail and dining concepts. What makes an area magical? What karma must exist in order to create a great, world-class location that people want to visit? Although I feel I have important insights into those answers, stakeholders around the arena have been and are continuing to focus on the topic of how to manage that growth. What could the neighboring area look like? Who would go there? What can bring people there? What do people enjoy in public spaces? What supportive infrastructure is needed? How can it be a seamless location? What do people value? What are their needs? These are just a few of the questions that this group will be addressing. How do you go about the process?

Working in Charlotte for 19 months has given me the belief that this is a can-do community of individuals that enjoy the challenge of trying to make things great. Center City Partners has served all of us well as the rallying point for forward-thinking planning. Not only have nationally and internationally acclaimed experts been attacking these issues to date, but local and national urban planners are now fine-tuning these early and preliminary concepts.

As a sports facility executive for more than 30 years, I have seen some instances in which these areas have proven to be incredibly successful and others that have been boringly dull and lifeless. I have spent the last ten years participating in a plethora of seminars in which best practices, best concepts and best projects are presented by all types of consultants, architects, retailers, and sports executives. The common threads among the great successes are that they are seamlessly integrated not only physically but psychically with their own cities. What works in one city stylistically cannot automatically be replicated in another city. In the sports world, we use the reference of an offense that takes what the defense gives you. A successful plan in Charlotte has to embrace these concepts in its own unique way.

That's what I have been thinking about ever since I started my job with the Bobcats. Look to these cities that have done it right: San Francisco, San Diego, Denver, and Baltimore with their baseball stadia. When you visit, you can see the contiguous development and vibrancy that is in the air. We have an incredibly unique opportunity at hand. All great ideas are welcome. Let's hear yours. ⏻

Favorite Things
March 2005

- The St. Patrick's Day Parade
- Blis Uptown Gift Shop
- SoHo Bistro
- Charlotte Art League
- The Sandwich Club

IS THE 2010 VISION REAL?

BY DAN THILO, URBAN DESIGN PROGRAM MANAGER,
CHARLOTTE-MECKLENBURG PLANNING COMMISSION

JANUARY 2006

In 2000, the City, the County and Charlotte Center City Partners sponsored the 2010 Center City Vision Plan. Inevitably, someone will ask: Is it real? Will it come true? Can we rely upon it? Does it really impact what happens on the ground?

The 2010 Plan represented the evolution of city planning over four decades. In the 1960s and 1970s, after urban renewal when downtown had become abandoned, our concern was making the core of the city viable. In the 1980s and 1990s, with the rejuvenation of Fourth Ward and the growth of our major employers, we concentrated on making Uptown livable. In 2000, as we considered the thousands of new residents moving into the city, we turned our attention to making the heart of the city memorable.

But does community envisioning work? A closer look into the vision or master plan might help answer the question.

In Charlotte, strategic plans for the urban core have been updated on a ten year cycle. Prior to the 2010 Plan, plans were the result of the collaboration of a select group of business and government leaders determined to meet the needs inside the freeway loop. For several months they would huddle to create a plan with solutions to stop the outgoing flight of business and residents to the suburbs. Urban design ordinances were written, streetscape improvements were made, and ground work laid to entice businesses to stay. The ambiance of the area became viable for the nine-to-five office workers. What lacked was energy beyond the work day.

In 2000, we took an entirely new approach to generating a common vision. The magic ingredient was people. People of all walks of life participated in determining what the vision should be and the necessary elements needed to make it successful. Large public meetings gave citizens the opportunity to voice their wishes. Citizens wanted parks, entertainment and art venues, transportation alternatives and a range of housing. The Center City boundary was expanded to include adjacent neighborhoods. The vision stretched beyond the parameters of previous thinking. People cited a desire for a center city that provided the necessities to live, work and play. In addition, they felt new catalyst projects were needed to leave a lasting impression on those who visit.

Their vision included an urban arena, a multi-modal transportation center, and covering a segment of the John Belk Freeway to provide pedestrian access to South End, an urban mixed-use-village in First Ward, the restoration of a residential neighborhood in Second Ward, creating an urban academic campus, and developing a large urban park. Citizens felt these were the missing pieces that would combine to make the Center City a place to remember – a place people wanted to be. The list was a list for all of Charlotte.

That was five years ago. In just five years, the fruits of the community visioning are blooming. We have a new arena, planning for a new multi-modal station is underway, a new park is in the design stage, baseball is being reviewed, new high-rise residential buildings are abounding, NASCAR is considering Charlotte for its Hall of Fame, Johnson & Wales University is educating students, a master plan for the rejuvenation of Second Ward has been completed, a Center City Transportation Plan is nearing completion and a new mixed-use art/theater complex is in the design stage on South Tryon. In five years, with the major exception of capping the freeway, nearly 90% of the ideas dreamed about during the 2010 visioning are being realized.

The Plan was a vision for what people wanted, not necessarily the details of how it would happen. Although the Plan envisioned location of facilities, land ownership, financing and unforeseen land use changes often determine placement. The Plan solidifies the principle that the Center City is the core of the entire region, providing a synergy of amenities for everyone. City leaders, private corporations and citizens worked together to achieve a dream. As the Center City 2010 Vision Plan edges past half way on its completion timeline, the vast majority of the goals have been accomplished and success seems imminent.

Is the 2010 vision real? It is because people in Charlotte have strived to involve everyone to make it possible. Imagine what 2020 will bring. ⏻

Q&A with Hunter Widener

By Mark Peres

September 2004

Hunter Widener is a Vice President/Private Client Manager in the Bank of America Private Bank. He serves on the Board of Directors of Hands On Charlotte and is an Alumni Council officer of Charlotte Country Day School. Hunter is the 2005 Chair of The Charlotte City Committee, a non-profit organization of emerging leaders in the Charlotte region. The City Committee has recently launched an initiative to fashion Charlotte a "Cool Community."

Tell us about The Charlotte City Committee.

The Charlotte City Committee is an inclusive, diverse, action-based group of emerging leaders that is working collaboratively with Charlotte's business executives, community leaders and elected officials to position Charlotte as the best place to live and work in America. The Committee was founded in October 2002 as a direct result of an inter-city visit to Indianapolis by the Charlotte Chamber of Commerce. We recognized that senior leadership in Charlotte is becoming overburdened. We need to identify, develop, engage and support some "bench strength" to support our current leaders. As Charlotte evolves, we must develop more civic and business leaders. One of the Committee's greatest accomplishments to date is having built a pool of emerging leaders with a great capacity to serve. We currently have 68 members.

What is the "Cool Community" initiative?

It is an initiative to measure and improve our "cool" factor as a region in order to attract and retain a talented and knowledgeable workforce and citizenry. Our community is experiencing rapid change and demographic shifts in the workplace. Over the next few years, we will be faced with the exiting of the baby boomers from the workforce, increased competition for young, creative talent, and an influx of minority talent that will cause a marked change in the complexion and culture of the Greater Charlotte region. Understanding and embracing these changes is critical for us to remain competitive as we position the region for the future.

How will you measure success?

Success will be measured by (1) an improved perception among Greater Charlotte's young professionals of the region's "coolness"; (2) an increase in the number of local, regional and national media outlets that put "Greater Charlotte" and "cool" or "hip" in the same article or story; (3) Greater Charlotte's employers self-report their increased ability to attract and retain talent; (4) a net in-flow of Generation Xers to Greater Charlotte in the next county labor market census; and (5) a self-reported "boost" or greater ROI in region-wide collaboration in attracting and retaining talent. ⏻

TICKET TO RIDE

BY JILL WALKER, CHARLOTTE VIEWPOINT COLUMNIST

JANUARY 2005

As in the children's book, *The Little Engine That Could*, advocates for a light rail system in Charlotte will reach the crest of a troublesome journey in early 2007 (fingers crossed) to the chant of "I knew we could, I knew we could, I knew we could."

That is when the South Corridor Light Rail Project is scheduled for completion. Costing at least $400 million, the South Corridor light rail represents one spoke of the city's five corridor 20-year transit plan, which has a current cost estimate of six billion dollars.

Let's face it, there are numerous reasons to be skeptical about a train that will run up and down South Boulevard all day, from I-485 (where the Carolina Pavilion big boxes are) to Seventh Street. And they've been articulated by many people over the last couple of years, most notably *Creative Loafing's* Tara Servatius, who, among other topics, explored the two consulting firms chosen to oversee our light rail and mass transit plan. Suffice it to say, they also oversaw Boston's infamous "Big Dig" project.

Introducing light rail in Charlotte now is akin to performing plastic surgery on a 35-year-old. Too much too soon. But oh boy, wait ten or so years and the benefits will bring a smile to your face, without all the lines. There really isn't a perfect time to introduce light rail to a city. Too early and everybody questions why, too late and the land costs are so prohibitive everybody questions why you waited so long.

Light rail on the south corridor won't solve all of our traffic problems. In fact, it probably won't solve any of them. What it will do, or what it can do is chart a different course for our future. If it is accompanied by the promised organic urban enclave spelled out in the South End Pedscape/Transit Station Area Plan, then it will begin to respond to some growing trends and needs in the city of Charlotte.

Most importantly, the development spurred by light rail can greatly expand housing options for many growing segments of our population. Access to affordable housing where a car is not required would benefit many of Charlotte's lower-waged citizens. Surveys of older people, empty nesters and young "creatives" indicate a strong preference for access to mass transit, as well as 18-hour neighborhoods that have a sense of place.

The city is encouraging population density in the vicinity of all the transit stations. Transit-oriented development, or TOD, is the comprehensive approach to this effort. The success of light rail lies solely on occupancy rates, so it is no surprise that the city will do everything in its power to assure that the trains are filled. Ergo, TOD, which involves government enhancements to a neighborhood, some developer incentives and a new TOD zoning classification.

As of now, properties within 1/2 mile of a transit station will be rezoned TOD. An unusual aspect of TOD zoning is that it sets minimums for density requirements and maximums for parking requirements. For instance, a residential structure must have a minimum of 15 units per acre and a maximum of 1.6 parking spaces per unit. While this might seem innocuous, it does open the door to very large scale projects that possibly won't have adequate parking. Why would a developer provide 1.6 spaces per unit if he/she can get away with less? And why build 15 units per acre if 90 can fit?

Scale is critical to the success of this new development. Perhaps the city needs to tighten some of these guidelines surrounding TOD, or phase in some of the minimum and maximum requirements, in order to preserve the existing residential character of the surrounding neighborhoods. And, if developers will get a free ride on parking, why not explore return compensations from them, like contributions to public art or transit passes to residents?

Despite all this, light rail and the new urban development that will accompany it, could be just what Charlotte needs. And, who knows, someday it might just entice my son back from Hoboken, where he took his recent college degree, big dreams and starting salary, and bought himself a subway ticket. ⏻

Q&A with Chuck Richards

By Jaime Bedrin

March 2004

Chuck Richards is owner of Reid's Fine Foods located at the Seventh Street Station in First Ward. J. Arthur Reid opened the original Reid's meat and dry goods store on Providence Road in 1928. Chuck, who began working at Reid's in 1961, became owner in 1984. He opened the Uptown store in 1998.

Why did you decide to locate Reid's Uptown?

When we evaluated whether or not to open an Uptown location for Reid's, we looked at where we wanted to be in 10 years, and the opportunity for growth in Uptown was just too good to pass up. It's true that opening in Seventh Street Station was a bit of a pioneer effort given the size of the Uptown population at the time, but it also gave us the opportunity to choose the best location.

How has the property around Reid's changed in the time since you opened?

We knew the Trolley was coming our way, and had an idea the Children's Learning Center might be built. But with the new arena out our side door and the emergence of light rail stopping at our front door, things have come together nicely. Also, the interest in living Uptown has exploded, so we are continuing to see projects develop that strengthen our position.

How did you feel about Harris Teeter opening an Uptown market?

We viewed it as a reinforcement of what we had been saying for several years – Uptown is a great place to live, work and play. We both bring things to the table.

How have your customers' needs changed since you first opened?

Prior to opening, we had no less than six focus group sessions to ask our potential customers what they wanted in a grocery store. Since opening, we have reset the entire store at least three times and almost doubled the number of product offerings. Because we are locally owned, we can make adjustments quickly to conform to the wants and needs of our customers.

What's next for Reid's?

We will continue to work closely with our neighbors to make the shopping experience at Reid's very special. We've set our bar very high. We challenge ourselves to serve our customers better and better each day. We want to set the standard for excellent service in Charlotte. ⏻

POSITIVE ENERGY
BY CARROLL GRAY, PRESIDENT, CHARLOTTE CHAMBER OF COMMERCE

JULY 2005

When I arrived in Charlotte in 1984 from Greenville, South Carolina, to serve as president of the Charlotte Chamber of Commerce, Charlotte was looking to be "someone." It was a young city working to establish its presence, both regionally and nationally, and wanted desperately to become known for something.

If you look at all of the hand-wringing these days about branding our city, you might wonder what has changed. But, in my 20-plus years as Chamber president, I'll tell you that Charlotte has become that "someone." While it might not be as glamorous as Hollywood or as sexy as being the city by the bay, Charlotte is known throughout the nation for its ability to implement public-private partnerships to get things done.

Whether it was an elite group of five business leaders locked in a corporate boardroom 20 years ago deciding that Charlotte needed to aggressively recruit the Piedmont Air hub to Charlotte/Douglas Airport, or whether it's a diverse group of civic, business and government leaders working to solve today's ozone challenges, Charlotteans have always worked together across political and social lines – to accomplish civic goals.

While it seems second nature for us to work together, the kind of public-private partnerships we take for granted in Charlotte-Mecklenburg are the same kind that other communities of our size marvel at.

People often ask me about Charlotte's competitive advantages. While we favorably compare to cities we compete with for economic development projects on things like location, taxes, and cost of living, what really sets Charlotte apart from these communities is its ability to forge partnerships, and its cohesive civic spirit: what we refer to through our economic development campaign as "positive energy." It's that positive energy that distinguishes a great city from a good one.

But as Charlotte diversifies, this cohesive civic spirit is beginning to fray, threatening the region's positive energy and the progress we've made. Too many people – even those in our own region, who choose to live, work and play here – are willing to tear down the spirit of our community without offering constructive suggestions on how to make systemic changes to the very items they're complaining about.

Yes, our city has challenges. Education could be our Achilles' heel. But we've created a public-private partnership to work on those challenges: a private task force that will report back to public officials on recommendations for what could potentially be sweeping change in how our school system is structured.

The environment, particularly ozone and air quality, have us facing an end to federal transportation money if these challenges are not solved post haste. We've put together a public-private partnership, called Cutting Pollution When It Counts, that is looking at ways to get businesses to voluntarily commit to changing commuting patterns of their employees on high ozone days. Those alternate commuting plans are turned into the county so that county staff can track whether or not this voluntary program is making a difference in air quality.

But Charlotte has always been open to new people and new ideas. It's one of our city's greatest strengths. There is always room at the table for those with constructive, creative ideas that will help solve our city's issues.

But these days, there are often vacant seats at those decision-making tables. Instead of pitching in to help, those who criticize and complain the loudest stand back and wait for the calvary of established leaders to ride in on white horses and fix our city's problems, only to then criticize the solution we've come up with, or the process in which the solution was decided, or the personalities and pedigrees of the people who stepped up to make the decision.

Civic accomplishment is a confluence of leadership, by private individuals as well as elected officials. When you are frustrated with a city issue, it's easy to stand idly by, Monday morning quarterbacking those who have the courage to take the reins and make decisions. But it takes leadership and civic strength to offer workable solutions to problems. It's time we did much more of the latter, and less of the former. ⏻

Eavesdropping

Hot to the touch

Barebones theater

A Center City High School

By Rev. Dr. Louis "Smokey" Oats,
Headmaster, Trinity Episcopal School

December 2003

What about high school? Since arriving in 1999 to start a K-8 elementary school in First Ward, I've led dozens of presentations to prospective parents. At every one of them, someone has asked: "When are you going to start a high school?"

My standard answer is: "The Board of Trustees has declared that kindergarten through eighth grade is the ONLY school it is interested in launching. Someone else will have to initiate a high school." Make no mistake, Charlotte is blessed with a number of outstanding high schools, both public and private. Their campuses offer wonderfully comprehensive programs of rigorous academics, vital life lessons and competitive sports. And to date, there is adequate room in them for admission of students from such schools as mine.

Still, as good as these high schools are, each of apparent necessity is a self-contained "ivory tower." They are self-reliant, independent, and largely disconnected from the economies and ecosystems that surround them. Other than the occasional field trip, students at these high schools do not know firsthand the joy and excitement, the opportunity and engagement, the vibrancy and energy of learning, living and loving in Uptown Charlotte.

A high school in the Center City would have all four wards as its campus. Imagine the life lessons and degree of learning in economics by observing deals being made on the Bank of America trading floor; in law by watching proceedings from the back row of the courtroom; in theatre arts by talking to stagehands as they erect the next set at the Blumenthal; in science by taking advanced classes at nearby CPCC or observing surgery at Presbyterian Hospital; in civics by attending planning commission committee hearings; in criminal justice by joining in on the change of shifts at the Uptown police headquarters; or in technology by visiting Gateway Village.

In a community where less than a third of the populace vote, where a national study has flagged the city for poor race relations, where disparity between the haves and have-nots is widening, a different, far more 'hands-on' and integrated approach to education would be a welcome change and of great benefit to all of Charlotte. A Center City High School would allow us to raise up a different kind of student and new kind of leader. ⏻

Q&A with Moira Quinn

By Jaime Bedrin

December 2003

Moira Quinn is Senior Vice President of Communications and COO for Charlotte Center City Partners, which is dedicated to the enhancement of business, cultural, retail and residential initiatives in Charlotte's central business district.

You hold an important position with CCCP, but you are also very involved with Temple Beth-El. How do you manage work, life and family?

I've tried to choose a few extra-curricular activities and do them well. The great thing about Temple Beth-El is that much of what I do there is with the family. We go to services and participate in Mitzvah projects together. My son, David, said I could only serve on the Temple Board of Directors if I promised to attend ONE meeting a month. After all, I already sing with the choir once a week. So far, I'm doing pretty well with that promise!

Are there lessons from working with the Temple that carry over to CCCP?

It's interesting, there are a surprising number of parallels between the work I do with the Temple and CCCP. Both are non-profits with identical budgets. The job I have at CCCP is essentially the same as the Temple Executive Director. For CCCP, I'm staff, working with a very strong Board...for the Temple, I'm part of a very strong Board, working with staff. I have specific ideas about the way boards and staff interact. In both, character, honesty, trust and willingness to leap in with both feet and just do the job is key.

What do you do with your spare time?

Spare time? HAH! Actually, I love to read in the tub...that's the ultimate treat. I love to sing, so singing with the choir is recreation for me. And my son, David, and I bake bread from scratch. I've also decided to take up knitting. If you knit, you can do something else at the same time...the perfect hobby for me!

You have deep roots in Charlotte. What's your vision for the future of the Center City?

I think it's vital to have a strong urban core. The Center City is the economic engine of Charlotte...it's the heart of the city. A city has to be strong from the ground up. We push hard to animate the streets, to spur street-level shopping and activity. The new arena and Johnson & Wales are going to change the landscape. My vision is more retail, more rooftops and more animation on the streets. Charlotte is on a roll, and is going to keep on rolling. ⏻

Q&A with Henry Bostic

By Mark Peres

December 2004

Henry Bostic serves on the Steering Committee of the Mecklenburg Status of Seniors Initiative and is chair of the Initiative's public relations committee. He became interested in senior issues while he headed the Western Carolina Chapter of the Alzheimer's Association. Henry has lived in Charlotte since 1970 and has been involved primarily in health care non-profits. Today he has his own public relations and non-profit consulting firm – Bostic and Associates.

What is the Status of Seniors Initiative?

The Initiative is a community-based, on-going strategic planning effort to improve the lives of older adults in Charlotte-Mecklenburg. Its aims are to promote awareness of the coming surge in the senior population and to develop recommendations to the entire community for changes and improvements that will encompass all areas of senior adults' lives. Since May 2004, volunteers have presented the United Way, the County Commissioners, the City Council and numerous community and civic groups the first fruits of their efforts – a 280-page report packed full of vital information concerning the coming increase in the senior population. The report contains seven broad recommendations. The full report and other information about the Initiative are available on the Web and copies of the full report are available in every library branch.

How did the Initiative come about?

In May 2003, the Human Services Council presented the Mecklenburg Board of County Commissioners (BOCC) a "Status of Seniors" report that the BOCC had requested a year earlier. The report estimates that the more than 80,000 people 60 and older living in the county today will nearly triple by 2025 when the oldest of the Baby Boomers turn 79. Not only will the surge in older citizens significantly increase demand for senior services, but it will alter traditional ways of doing business. Experts say a labor shortage is all but inevitable as the boomers begin to retire. A National Association of Manufacturers news release forecasts that a skilled worker gap will begin in 2005 and grow to 5.3 million by 2010 and 14 million by 2020. Preparing for the expected population growth even seven years out when the first of the Baby Boomers reach 65 is something the community must address now, the report concluded, if we can hope to get ahead of the curve.

Why is the Initiative important?

More people are alive today who are 65 or older than ever before in our nation's history. But we haven't seen anything yet. In 1960, only one American in 10 was 65 or older. Today, that ratio is about one in eight, and it will reach one in six within 30 years. Charlotte-Mecklenburg must be ready for a time in the not-too-distant future when there will be only two workers for each retiree over age 65.

Is a senior-friendly community out of step with a city intent on attracting a young creative class?

Certainly not. Becoming a "senior-friendly community" simply means that our community will provide a wide range of social and economic opportunities and support for all citizens. It means we value seniors' contributions, we promote positive intergenerational relations, we consider the needs and interests of seniors in our planning, we respect and support seniors' desire to live independently and we acknowledge the primary role that families, friends and neighbors play in sustaining older adults. The Carolinas have become one of the leading retirement destinations. Part of our appeal is in our weather and our cost of living. Another reason is that more and more parents are moving to the greater Charlotte area to be close to their children and their grandchildren. For our community to be as attractive as it can be to any age group, it must be attractive to all age groups.

How can citizens help?

The Status of Seniors Initiative is a volunteer driven effort. We welcome anyone who wants to help develop ideas and strategies to ensure that Mecklenburg County becomes an even more senior-friendly community. ⏻

THE MINT MUSEUMS
BY PHIL KLINE, EXECUTIVE DIRECTOR OF THE MINT MUSEUMS

SEPTEMBER 2005

The Mint Museums are the region's premier visual arts museums, with an impressive history of community service, and the potential for dramatically increasing the ability to deliver exceptional exhibitions and education programming through the expansion plans now underway. The Mint Museum of Art opened as North Carolina's first art museum in 1936 and underwent major expansions in 1967 and 1985. The Mint Museum of Craft + Design opened in 1999 after Bank of America's generous donation of a building. The Museums are collecting institutions with more than 28,000 art works that are held as part of our public trust to the community. Artistic focus areas are American Art (notably the work of Romare Bearden), Ceramics, Contemporary Art, Contemporary Craft, Historic Costume and Pre-Columbian Art.

Exhibitions of the collection are complemented by national touring exhibitions, which allow us to bring art works that would not otherwise be available to the community. This fall we will continue the tradition of great traveling exhibitions with Renaissance to Rococo: Masterpieces from the Collection of the Wadsworth Anthenum Museum of Art at the Art Museum and Don Reitz: Clay, Fire, Salt and Wood at the Craft + Design Museum. Exhibitions are supported by award-winning education programs that serve all ages from pre-school to seniors. For example every fifth-grade public school student and many private school students participate in a curriculum-based program Deciphering and Investigating Great Societies (DIGS) that utilizes our outstanding Pre-Columbian collection. Program opportunities and more information can be found at our website: www.mintmuseum.org.

The Mint Museums are a component of the Cultural Facilities Plan that is being coordinated by the Arts & Science Council with support from the private sector and elected officials of the Charlotte City Council and the Mecklenburg Board of County Commissioners. The proposal for The Mint Museums will allow us to gain the critically needed space for galleries, education programs, visitor services and storage.

Wachovia has generously offered to include the proposed new Center City art museum of The Mint Museums in a mixed-used development on South Tryon Street. Bank of America has also stepped forward to support this proposal by offering to buy the current Craft + Design building. This wonderful collaboration will allow The Mint Museums to gain the much-needed incremental space while co-locating the Craft + Design collection with the new museum thus enhancing the visitor's experience through expanded offerings.

The new Center City museum will include the artistic focus areas of American Art including African American Art, Contemporary Art and Contemporary Craft as well as African Art and European Art. The museum will also host many of the major traveling exhibitions and will create the opportunity to bring larger exhibitions both in terms of number and scale of works. The Mint Museum of Art will continue to operate at the Randolph Road site focusing on the collection areas of Ceramics, Historic Costume and Pre-Columbian Art along with Spanish Colonial, Coins and Currency and Asian Art. Each of the artistic focus areas have strong support groups and associated education programs to ensure their continued success.

Planning for the new museum is underway to create wonderful experiences for our visitors. The increased gallery space will allow the display of more of the permanent collection in addition to providing a venue for expanded offerings of national and international exhibitions. Expanded educational space will support increased programming to better serve the community. Visitor services will be enhanced with a café, retail shop, library, auditorium, coatroom and event space that either does not currently exist or is limited.

The Mint Museums are committed to providing the community with the opportunity to view incredible works through both our permanent collection presentations and touring exhibitions from other major institutions. We are equally committed to offering programming to engage all ages in the ability to learn and appreciate the impact of the visual arts.

The Mint Museums are supported by a dedicated staff, an engaged Board of Trustees and Advisory Board, an Arts & Science Council, individual and corporate sponsors, and eight affiliate groups with more than 2,200 members. We encourage you to visit the Museums to enjoy the rewarding experience of the visual arts! ⏻

FAVORITE THINGS

October 2005

- The Biltmore Croissant at Reid's
- Cosmos Café
- Novello Festival of Reading
- CVS on North Graham
- The StoryJar at ImaginOn

PUBLIC ART, ACCOMPLISHED KIDS
By Dennis Marsoun, Charlotte ViewPoint Columnist

May 2005

We're about to get a new headquarters in Uptown Charlotte. Not a major corporation, not a new banking division, and not an Internet dot.com start-up. This will be a headquarters for KIDS! ImaginOn, the Joe & Joan Martin Center, a joint venture of The Public Library of Charlotte & Mecklenburg County and the Children's Theater of Charlotte, is transforming a city block that used to contain three parking lots and an abandoned building into something truly special.

Why Uptown for this center? It is not uncommon to see kids of all ages being herded towards Discovery Place, sometimes holding onto rope, to see an exhibit like Sue, the T-Rex currently on display. Yellow school buses vie for position to load and unload kids – quite something to see in a buttoned-up town. It's magic for kids to go where their parents go – only without them. I remember growing up in Cleveland, Ohio, and how I would love to go downtown for parades or with my mom to shop at one of the department stores, Higbee's, Halle's or The May Company. It was, in my way, my introduction to public art as well. The Soldiers and Sailors Monument took a central position on Public Square, and contained both statues of naval heroes and soldiers ready for action. There was also a gallery inside with paintings of famous battles.

As impressive as that was, it was no match for the public art located throughout Charlotte, whether the mobiles in the Carillon Building, frescoes in the Bank of America Corporate Center or the Trans-America Building, the water falling front of the Interstate Tower, the ceramic birdhouses in Fourth Ward, or the book motif on The Green. ImaginOn will be a form of public art as well. Located a block away from the new arena site, and adjacent to the Trolley/Light Rail line, it will be festooned with art from accomplished artists and accomplished kids. Much of the art will be performance art, but art by any name is art.

ImaginOn is no minor effort. There will be two theaters within the building – one rising four stories off the ground will hold 550 people, and a second, more intimate theater will embrace 250 people. There will be a technology center, classrooms, library areas, story time rooms, and a special section just for teenagers as well. If you haven't seen it grow, take some time, and you will be amazed at what's happening. ⏻

What I've Learned

By Dr. Peter Gorman, Superintendent,
Charlotte-Mecklenburg Schools

August 2006

As I have met community members, parents and CMS staff during my first few weeks on the job, I have been struck by the intensity of feeling and the diversity of opin-ions about our schools and what needs to be done next to improve them. This district is fortunate – and remarkable – in the intense level of community interest we have.

It's clear that this community is passionate about education and wants something done, now. The public's trust in CMS has become frayed, and we need time to put some needed reforms in place. This we will do, using a simple three-question standard to evaluate our actions: Is it good for kids? Is it educationally sound? Is it fiscally responsible?

Despite that fraying of trust, I have faith that our diverse and sometimes fractious community can pull together if individuals are willing to focus on what unites us, rather than on what divides us. And what unites us is a deep commitment to a strong public education system, one that promotes both equity and excellence.

Part of that commitment is making sure that our school facilities are adequate. The simple truth is: right now, they're not. The needs of this school system are undeniable. We already have more than 20,000 children in mobile classrooms. We expect to gain 4,400 new students in August, bringing the total number of CMS students this year to more than 128,000. To educate them, and educate them well, we need new schools and we need to renovate and expand some existing facilities.

And because we're a county-wide system, we have the full range of capital issues confronting us. Relieving overcrowding in the suburbs is desperately needed. High school students shouldn't have to carry 45 pounds of books in their backpacks all day long because their school is too crowded or too sprawling to give them regular access to a locker. Elementary school children shouldn't have to eat lunch at 10:30 a.m. and the quality of our school facilities shouldn't reflect a child's zip code.

Principle – setting aside our individual preferences to meet the larger educational good – demands that we do something now to start meeting the needs of our children. True leadership often requires compromise. We cannot mistake preference for principle. As parents, we don't want to stand on principle and do nothing, or proudly vote no – only to have to go home and say to our children, "I stood my ground, I voted on principle, but I failed you."

I believe the recommendation to pursue a bond package next year, using citizen input to develop specific projects and recommendations, is a wise one. We need to balance not falling further behind in construction while building trust and support. We have already seen one bond issue fail. CMS cannot afford another such failure, and it also can't afford to wait much longer to address the very real, very critical capital issues. The time for us as a com-munity to come together and start building a coalition to support the school bonds package is now, not a year from now.

This community is both broad and diverse – we have banking leaders, faith leaders, community leaders, sports enterprises – the list goes on and on. All of these groups need to help in the effort to get the word out that Charlotte-Mecklenburg Schools are at a critical juncture. If we don't build some new schools and renovate the ones we have, we are only going to fall farther behind.

This community prides itself on outstanding schools. It was the first city to successfully use busing to end segregation – it was a national model for how it handled such a difficult issue. We have millions of dollars in scholarship money – some of it from the best universities in America – flowing to our graduating seniors each year. This is a good school system, and my goal for it is that it not merely stay good, but get better. To get there, we need capital improvements and a bond issue.

I urge all of the city's many leaders and many communities to come together and help us make this happen. If we fail this time, we will have failed our children and their future. . ⏻

Q & A with Emily Zimmern

by Jennifer Garner

June 2006

Emily Zimmern has served as executive director of the Levine Museum of the New South since March 1995. A native of Louisiana, she earned her B.A. and M.A. in American history from Vanderbilt University, and an M.B.A. from Queens College. She has held numerous leadership positions in local and national nonprofit organizations including United Jewish Appeal, Charlotte Jewish Federation, Foundation for the Carolinas, Crisis Assistance Ministry and Planned Parenthood. Zimmern is a graduate of Leadership Charlotte and the American Leadership Forum, Charlotte Chapter. She currently serves on the Mayor's International Cabinet and the Visitors Advisory Council of the Charlotte Regional Visitors Authority. Honors include Charlotte Woman of the Year 2002 and a Charlotte Business Journal *Women in Business Achievement Award for 2003.*

Why do we need a museum of the New South?

Charlotte has a wonderful collection of sites and facilities that preserve and chronicle our Southern heritage. Prior to the Levine Museum of the New South, we didn't have an organization that was interpreting our recent history for the public. Charlotte really is a product of the New South; at the time of the Civil War, Charlotte was just an upstart village of a few thousand people. Our growth was really post-1865 and continues today. There is an incredible amount of scholarship being done on the New South at area colleges, and the Levine Museum allowed us the venue and programs to bring this history to the citizens of the Charlotte area and the thousands of visitors to this area every year. Our permanent exhibit, "Cotton Fields to Skyscrapers" is one of the most comprehensive exhibits in the nation on the history of the New South and was funded in part by the National Endowment for the Humanities.

The "Courage" exhibit on the school desegregation lawsuit received a lot of attention in Charlotte, what kind of long-term effects did that create?

The "Courage" exhibit was a phenomenal success. We used the exhibit to create civic dialogue about a difficult subject. One program brought management teams through the exhibit, followed by a guided dialogue through our partnership with the Community Building Initiative. We created a safe environment for people to discuss these issues and brought over 1,700 people through that program. The "Courage" exhibit won several national awards, including the National Museum Service Award, which was presented by the First Lady at the White House to the Levine Museum. We would like to build on this kind of community dialogue with future exhibits.

How do you make Charlotte's history relevant to those citizens whose history is not that of the South?

We are partnering with Mecklenburg Ministries to create another community dialogue program around our upcoming exhibit on "The Families of Abraham" and the history of Christian, Jewish and Muslim faiths in Charlotte. We are also focusing on the newest citizens of the New South, those who have moved here from other countries and bring their rich and diverse heritages with them. We want to use history's lessons to build community between the diverse groups that make up the New South today. We are developing exhibits around the Cambodian and Latino communities in Charlotte and are excited about these upcoming events. Already all CMS eighth graders come to the museum as one of their required field trips. We have several exhibits that are currently on the road and bringing Southern history to new audiences. We received a grant from Bank of America to take part of the "Courage" exhibit to New York City, Washington D.C., and Atlanta. The grant will also help to house the exhibit in a permanent location in Charlotte.

Our exhibit on the architect of Myers Park, John Nolen, has also traveled around Charlotte and Mecklenburg County. Part of the "Courage" exhibit even went to Johannesburg, South Africa. Our programs on "New South for New Southerners" and "Global Dish" have provided fun, short evening programs designed to welcome newcomers to Charlotte and learn about our history, culture and cuisine. We are also going to conduct a "New South barbecue" bus tour as part of "Charlotte Shout" again this fall as a way to visit the many kinds of restaurants around town with an international and traditional twist to Southern barbecue. We will also repeat our popular Gospel Shout program. We hope that these diverse programs will bring new visitors and guests to the museum.

How do you think your location uptown has been important to the mission of the museum?

I have to thank our earlier board members for the decision to locate in the Center City. When we moved into this building in 1994, it was surrounded by a sea of parking lots. Today, we are in the heart of the Center City and love all the synergies between ImaginOn, the Arena, the trolley, uptown residents and dining. We love that we were part of the transition and growth of the Center City to the vibrant, diverse and dynamic area that it is now. While we plan to stay put in this space, we are going to be reaching an even broader audience through our traveling exhibits and outreach programs. ⏻

BREVARD

Q&A with Winn Maddrey III

By Mark Peres

January 2005

Winn Maddrey is president of Blue Nine Partners, a business advisory firm providing management and communications counsel, primarily to early-stage and middle-market companies. Winn has served in leadership roles at the Charlotte Chamber of Commerce, the Charlotte City Committee, the Arts & Science Council, and the United Way. He has helped launch several not-for-profit initiatives, including the Involvement Forum, the Impact Fund and Charlotte Convergence. He recently chaired a forum on business innovation in Charlotte.

How do you define business innovation?

Innovation means new ideas, new implementation and new execution in the marketplace as opposed to theory in the classroom.

Who are the innovative companies in Charlotte?

There are countless innovative companies in Charlotte. Innovation exits everywhere, from local companies such as LendingTree, Harris Teeter, Family Dollar, Harper's, Goodrich, Allen Tate, Goodmortgage, Reid's and countless others. But it is hard to quantify, because counting the number of patents is not a way that we can measure our companies in Charlotte.

Does Charlotte have the talent pool to support innovation?

Charlotte has a growing talent pool to meet the needs of small, medium and large businesses. Our universities are critical to generating talent. The better and more innovative our universities, the better and more innovative our companies will be. The good news is that the number and quality of graduates is growing – and Charlotte is becoming a place where these graduates want to live. The best assets we have for our future are UNC Charlotte, Queens, Johnson & Wales, Wake Forest and other premier higher education institutions.

How does Charlotte compare and contrast with other markets known for innovation?

A frequent comparison is made between the Triangle and Charlotte. The Triangle, which offers world-class education and approximately 18 colleges and universities, is known for innovation. If you asked someone nationally whether Charlotte is an innovation corridor, the answer would be no. Charlotte is perceived as a big company town. But if you look at the recruiting numbers, it tells a different story. In the past 10 years, the Charlotte Chamber has recruited more than 8,800 companies to this market with 75,926 jobs – an average of 8.6 employees per company. So growth in our marketplace, in terms of jobs, occurs at the smaller companies. And I believe innovation drives this dynamic.

What does Charlotte have to do to support innovation?

In addition to elevating and embracing research and entrepreneurship at our universities, we need to do two things. We need to actively mentor those who want to start or grow a business. If someone is successful in their career, that individual should mentor others who might follow in their footsteps. That is part of being an innovator. Connecting people to others who have similar interests… and recognizing similar talents. It helps people who are successful build other successful companies.

We also need to become more risk-tolerant of new ideas as it pertains to business start-ups, diverse points of view and emerging technologies. For example, if you meet two people at a cocktail party and one person says "I work at a bank" and the other says, "I work at a software company," the Charlotte marketplace sees banking as a smarter career choice.

Charlotte is used to slow, steady growing corporations, such as banks, retailers and utilities. There is nothing wrong with that, but Charlotte needs economic diversification. Charlotte is not yet a place for start-ups. If you look at the Triangle, embarking on an innovative career is viewed differently than in Charlotte. Our city needs to celebrate venturing as much as getting a job at a big company. ⏻

Q & A with Cynthia Marshall

By Mark Peres

August 2005

Cynthia Marshall has served as Executive Director of Communities In Schools of Charlotte-Mecklenburg, Inc., (CIS) since its founding in 1985. Prior to her work in organizing CIS, Cynthia was 1984-1985 President of the Junior League of Charlotte, a volunteer organization dedicated to training young women for service. Cynthia has served on the board of directors of Child Care Resources, The Family Center, the Children's Law Center and on the United Way Planning Council. Cynthia has received the Order of the Long Leaf Pine by Governor Hunt, the Charlotte Business Journal Business Woman of the Year Award, the YWCA Woman of the Year Award, and the Charlotte Woman of the Year Award. She received her B.A. in biology from UNC at Greensboro and an M.S. in Biology from the University of Pennsylvania.

What is Communities In Schools: Why and how did it come about?

Communities In Schools (CIS) was founded by visionary Bill Milliken in New York City in the early 1970s. It was then called Cities In Schools, and is now the nation's largest stay-in-school network, helping young people in 225 communities to stay in school, successfully learn, and prepare for life by connecting needed community resources with schools and individual students. CIS is guided by its belief that every child needs and deserves Five Basic Resources:

• A one-on-one relationship with a caring adult
• A safe place to learn and grow
• A healthy start – a healthy future
• A marketable skill to use upon graduation; and
• A chance to give back to peers and community

Locally, CIS of Charlotte-Mecklenburg, Inc. was founded in 1985 under the leadership of John A. Tate, Jr. (Jack Tate) and Ed Crutchfield, CEO of First Union. CIS is a formal partnership with Charlotte-Mecklenburg Schools (CMS) and the school principals in each of 24 schools. CIS was established here at the invitation of School Superintendent Dr. Jay Robinson (now deceased) as a response to the growing dropout problem in secondary schools in this county.

CIS is funded in part by the Mecklenburg County Commission, the United Way of Central Carolinas, the Charlotte Merchants Foundation, local corporations, individuals and foundations, communities of faith, as well as contracts with the local Workforce Development Board (Department of Labor), CMS and Smart Start of Mecklenburg County.

How does Communities In Schools go about its work: What do you do on the ground?

CIS takes a holistic approach to drop out prevention by addressing the barriers to education – the physical, emotional, and academic needs of children and families – through a wide range of tutoring, counseling and mentoring programs; cultural and community service activities; health screenings and access to health care; and advisement for post-secondary education, financial aid, college scholarships, and career services through its ThinkCOLLEGE® program.

CIS works to ensure that every CIS student graduates from high school and enters some form of post-secondary education or training or gainful employment. It builds a continuum of support by building personal relationships with students and following their progress from elementary to high school and beyond.

Each year CIS works to secure funding for a full-time site coordinator in eight elementary, eight middle and eight local high schools, each of whom builds relationships with 100-150 students and partners with school personnel and community agency professionals, who provide needed services and special programming at each school – removing barriers to learning, instilling hope and reinforcing the vision of graduation and life after high school.

Students are targeted for CIS support due to a variety of high-risk indicators, including school absenteeism, performing below grade level in reading and math, fragile family income, as well as health, mental health and family issues. Students in foster care or families receiving Temporary Aid to Needy Families (TANF) are referred to CIS staff by the Department of Social Services for special attention and programming.

The proof of our work lies in the numbers. In the last school year alone, 2,206 students (K-12) were served by CIS. Of these students, 99% stayed in school, 91% were promoted to the next grade level (1,832 promoted), 92% – or 171/185 of the high school seniors – became graduates – and 64 of these seniors received college scholarships totaling $91,792 in June of 2005.

A total of $511,794 in scholarships was awarded to 293 CIS graduates, including (freshmen and upperclassmen) at the end of the 2004-2005 school year, and currently they are attending 47 different colleges across the U. S. with 48 of the 293 in the UNC system. These private scholarships supplemented the federal Pell grants which each student was eligible to receive.

Some take issue with the notion that it takes a village to raise a child. What is your response?

Our children and grandchildren will determine the quality of life and economic stability of this community for all of us for the future – for TOMORROW. If each child leads a productive and satisfying life, everyone benefits. I believe that we have a personal and moral responsibility to cherish and to integrate ALL children into the life and economy of this community. We have a choice – to ensure that they are contributors to this community – or that they are a drain on our limited resources and tax dollars. If we consider that 80% of the prison inmates in NC are school dropouts and that the cost of prison per year is more than a year of education at Harvard University, do we really have a choice of which is more positive, more productive, more humane? Another perspective to consider is that it is in our self-interest to ensure that there are well-educated and caring citizens to care for us and our families as we age out of productivity. Finally, there is the "silent crisis" described by Thomas Friedman in his best seller, "The World Is Flat" – and we cannot ignore the need to inspire and support our youth to fill the desperately needed occupations such as teachers, medical personnel and technology-savvy employees.

How do you assess CMS today versus 20 years ago? What difference has Communities In Schools made?

We know that there are hundreds of CIS students who were potential dropouts but stayed in school and graduated – and many who continued their education and are back in Charlotte – contributing to the quality of life and economic strength of this community. One of these students graduated from Davidson College, now works for Wachovia and is studying for his MBA from Wake Forest. He is giving back as a passionate member of the local CIS Board of Directors. Two other CIS graduates who also finished college in North Carolina, are employees of CIS and working with students at Garinger High School. The circle is complete. People believing in and supporting children. It is simple yet difficult – but it works.

Very simply, children, youth, adults – all of us need to be connected in meaningful ways to other people to be successful. We are all hungry for COMMUNITY. In some cases, the pupil assignment plan may have increased the mobility of a highly mobile group of students and their families, who change their residence often because of economics, family instability and consequently, have few real roots in a neighborhood or community. Perhaps, some of us can remember attending school with the same friends for many years – building relationships with peers with teachers, adding to our sense of trust, security, and self-worth. CMS teachers have done a remarkable job, especially given all the additional roles we expect of them – father, mother, social worker, hall monitor, nurse, etc.

What is the future of Communities In Schools: How can citizens help?

CIS initiated its ThinkCOLLEGE program to demonstrate that IF campus tours, advisement and financial support related to post-secondary education were offered to "first generation" college students, they would take advantage of the opportunities and succeed. The demonstration project worked! Now it is time for a community Call to Action – to establish (and fund) a community scholarship fund for all Mecklenburg County students – so that with one voice, this community can say to ALL of our young people: "You CAN obtain postsecondary training and education for the jobs WE NEED to keep Charlotte strong and growing!"

We welcome the opportunity to set up additional scholarship funds – by families, by companies, by churches, such as the one established by Myers Park Presbyterian Church – its Patricia Fields Scholarship Fund – whereby academically and economically eligible students not only receive college scholarships, but are matched with a personal "church buddy" who becomes their friend and mentor throughout their college career.

We need adult mentors of all ages for all students – for individual students to help them improve in reading or math – and explore careers – and what it takes to get there. We also need groups of professionals, such as accountants and other financial professionals who would help families complete the Federal financial aid forms (FAFSA) in order to recevie the Federal Pell grant monies – primarily in February and early March of 2006 – workshops to be held at main and neighborhood branches of the Public Library.

We need college alumni who would help CIS host events for high school seniors or CIS college students who need networking opportunities in order to connect to jobs or additional training. We need partnership programs between high school students and elementary school students – peer to peer mentoring and tutoring – which is mutually beneficial and rewarding. ⏻

QUEEN CITY ANNIVERSARIES

BY JAIME BEDRIN, REPORTER/PRODUCER, WFAE

NOVEMBER 2003

Ever since childhood, I've wanted to leave home, work very hard and become successful. I equated achievement with independence. And even though I am attached to my family, I needed space.

In August 2001, a few months after my 25th birthday, I left New York City for Charlotte. I had just received my graduate degree in journalism, and I was planning to work as a reporter. Charlotte offered me my first professional radio job.

My family said our goodbyes over lunch at a neighborhood bistro. My mother held back tears when my father walked me to my '93 Honda. I hugged my parents and told them I would be fine in Charlotte. Besides, I had my cat, Nina, to keep me company, and cousins in Raleigh. I was only an hour away by plane. We could visit any time.

Eleven days later I realized just how far I was from home. At a little after 8 o'clock, September 11th, 2001, my parents called to tell me they had heard that an airplane had hit the World Trade Center. They were on a bus on their way into New York City, not far from the Lincoln Tunnel. I didn't think the incident was very serious, but since I am a reporter, I called into work anyway, and learned that the Pentagon was aflame. The news team scrambled to cover the biggest story of our lives. Some colleagues cried openly. I had been at work one week, and I was convinced that I'd never see my parents again.

I've been in Charlotte a little over two years and I've found the process of negotiating my success in the Queen City awkward. After all, every anniversary of 9/11 is an anniversary of my arrival.

Somehow, amidst the chaos of those first three months in Charlotte, I did manage to experience what I set out to do in the first place. Despite minor loneliness and a longing for my favorite brand of Friendship cottage cheese, I was succeeding in Charlotte as a reporter and as a woman.

My father tells me I'm lucky to have left Manhattan when I did, and I know he's right, but somehow there is still a part of me that feels uneasy enjoying my new life in Charlotte while friends and family back home struggle to make things right again. ⏻

Buddha's birthday

April candles

Burned to nothing

Q& A with Pamela Meister
By Mark Peres

January 2004

Pamela Meister is President and CEO of the Charlotte Museum of History. Prior to her move to Charlotte in April 2004, she spent six years in Atlanta as Director of Education and Interpretation for the Atlanta History Center. From 1990 through 1997, Meister worked extensively to provide professional training and technical assistance for museums throughout twelve southeastern states as executive director of the Southeastern Museums Conference, as a faculty member in the Cultural Resource Management Program of Southeastern Louisiana University, and as a member of the Louisiana Division of the Arts' Peer Assistance Network. Prior to her work with museums, Meister had a ten-year career as a theatrical designer, stage manager, and arts administrator in New Orleans, Los Angeles, Washington, D.C., and Atlanta. She holds a B.A. in Theatre with a minor in History from the University of New Orleans and a M.F.A. in Arts Management from the University of Georgia.

What's the point of a history museum in a city so focused on the future?

A future-focused town like Charlotte needs a museum of history even more than places like Savannah, Charleston or Richmond that celebrate their history and have many more tangible pieces of the past than we do in Charlotte. I believe that we need to examine the past in order to understand the present, and that planning for the future should be informed by a solid understanding of what has gone before. It seems to me that Charlotte has a short time horizon – conversations frequently seem to focus on "right now" and "the next big thing" and that there is little acknowledgement of past history or long-term consequences of our present actions.

Why is Charlotte so caught up in change and validation?

Charlotte is a city that seems to be hard-wired for change. Starting out as an intersection of Native American trade routes, the city willed itself into existence, with no natural feature such as a navigable river or mountain pass to make it a logical spot to build a city. In many ways, Charlotte served as a blank slate for generations of people to write their own ambitions and dreams on it, and has reinvented itself again and again. Charlotte is a city that embraces newcomers, but it is also a city that doesn't seem to have a strong, widely held vision of its future, and thus obsessively compares itself to other places and looks outward rather than inward for validation.

What lessons from our past would Charlotte benefit from remembering?

Charlotte's early European settlers skewed toward independent individualism and self-reliance. The Scots-Irish and Moravians were natural revolutionaries, and they built community and questioned authority. In some ways, Charlotte has become a city that defers to authority, and I believe that we would benefit from a healthy dose of that Scots-Irish independence. In more recent history, Charlotte has a record of urban redevelopment that has displaced communities and destroyed irreplaceable historic structures. We need to remember those lessons as the city continues to grow and develop, and be careful about deconstructing neighborhoods.

Is Charlotte on an upward or downward spiral?

Upward! I'm an optimist. We're in an amazing period of growth, but we must remember that in the midst of great wealth and prosperity there is still poverty, need and racial distrust. With the rapid expansion of Charlotte's physical boundaries, we run the risk of becoming polarized. However, I'm continually impressed with Charlotte's "can-do" spirit and the amazing amount of time and energy that Charlotteans devote to civic endeavors. Projects such as Crossroads Charlotte are bringing together a broad cross-section of active and engaged citizens who are thoughtfully working to create a bright future for our city.

How does the Charlotte Museum of History differ from the Levine Museum of the New South?

I believe that all history museums have the basic mission of using the past to understand the present and shape the future. This is true for The Charlotte Museum of History and the Levine, but we have very different facilities and styles. The Levine focuses on the New South from 1865 to the future, their Center City facility is very urban, and they are known for their adult programs that build community through dialogue. The Charlotte Museum of History interprets Charlotte from its earliest days through today. We are the only history museum in Charlotte that includes a modern museum building and a historic site – the 1774 Hezekiah Alexander Homesite, the oldest surviving structure in Mecklenburg County. Our eight-acre site is uniquely suited for living history programs – you can literally walk out of the Museum's back door and be transported 200 years into the past. Because of this, we present a great deal of programming for families, children, and outreach toward schools.

What are you working hard on these days?

We're working hard on raising our profile in the community. We want people to know the Museum as a resource on Charlotte history, as a center for community activity, and as an educator and connector providing engaging, immersive experiences for adults, children and families. We want the community to use our facilities to meet its needs, and we're tracking who is coming to the Museum. As the keeper and interpreter of three centuries of Charlotte history, we're always working on telling the stories of Charlotte from multiple viewpoints, and we're always on the lookout for objects and documents that will help us tell those stories. ⏻

Breathing Deeply

By Michael Carson, Charlotte ViewPoint Columnist

December 2003

According to the American Lung Association, Charlotte is the 10th most polluted metropolis in the country in terms of air quality. There are a number of factors why, but a major cause is traffic. Each morning and evening, swarms of automobiles make their way into and out of the city, and without reliable mass transit and the lack of incentives to car pool, we cannot expect it to change.

Recently, I experienced our poor air quality first hand. On a long afternoon run through each of the Uptown wards, I twice ran alongside I-277, and each time I struggled to "get my air." Fortunately, the buzzing of the cars kept me mesmerized, and I didn't focus on my shortness of breath. Despite the negative effects on our environment and health, a remarkable number of politicians and citizens favor expanding highways to accommodate higher volumes of cars and fail to focus on longer-term solutions.

Now, our city doesn't entirely lack foresight on this issue. In 1998, in conjunction with a number of local municipalities and citizen committees, Charlotte created a visionary transit plan (2025 Transit Land Use Plan) that called for the development of a light rail system, bus rapid transit, and a streetcar system that would stretch to many of the smaller surrounding cities and existing Charlotte developments. In addition, the city is looking to develop a number of Uptown parks that will help to diffuse the smog that often plagues our city.

Change – mainly because of cost – is slow in coming. Over a 25-year period, the transit plan is projected to cost over one billion dollars, and although a significant amount will be met by state and federal funding, a great deal of the costs will be shouldered by the City of Charlotte and Mecklenburg County. Twenty-five years seems like a long time to me. I am personally in favor of declaring a moratorium on highway expansion (but not maintenance) in and around our city and instead using those proceeds to accelerate mass transit. It may not be realistic, but I can always hope.

Until Charlotte's mass transit system becomes a reality, we can all help to improve the quality of air and life in Charlotte. More of us should consider finding alternative modes of transportation. Reasonable options include moving into or closer to Uptown, using CATS or driving in a carpool. Your lungs and mine will thank you. ⏻

Q&A WITH JEAN GREER
BY MARK PERES

OCTOBER 2005

Jean Greer joined the Arts and Science Council of Charlotte-Mecklenburg in March 2000 as Vice President for Public Art. Jean has led the completion of a Public Art Master Plan and passage of the one percent for art programs for the City of Charlotte and Mecklenburg County. She provides the oversight and management of a growing series of diverse new projects both public and private. Prior to her appointment at the ASC, Jean served as public art and design administrator for the Broward County Cultural Affairs Division in Ft. Lauderdale, Florida, where she developed one of the country's best-established public art programs. For over nine years, she managed major projects at the Ft. Lauderdale/Hollywood International Airport, Port Everglades, and the Broward Civic Arena, along with numerous libraries, streetscapes, parks and neighborhood redevelopments. A highly regarded practitioner in the field of public art, Jean currently serves as Chair of the Public Art Network Council policy board, the national professional organization affiliated with Americans for the Arts.

Tell us broadly about public art in Charlotte? What is the state of public art in the city?

Charlotte's public art program began in 1981 under the Charlotte-Mecklenburg Planning Commission and has been administered by the ASC since 1993. Over the course of 25 years, 70 artworks have been created throughout our community by means of City and County funding. With the leadership of Bank of America, Wachovia and other private donors, our Center City has been greatly enriched with another 40 artworks which offer residents and visitors a sense of Charlotte's vitality, civic pride and beauty. Compared to other cities with notable collections, such as Portland, Dallas and Phoenix, we are about 10 years behind where we need to be. This is partly due to the previous voluntary funding policy. I am encouraged because the future looks promising. The City and the County 1% for art ordinances now enable funding for artworks dispersed throughout the growing urban area as part of new construction. ASC is currently managing 33 projects and will complete more than 10 large projects this year. The CATS public art program, a separate program within the City of Charlotte, has commissioned 13 artists to create multiple works for the 15 stations along the South Corridor in addition to 12 other works. So we are on the move!

What is the role of public art? Should it reflect or challenge community taste?

Public art can delight, engage, intrigue or challenge viewers. Artists as creators record and interpret who we are as a culture. Their artworks animate our community by adding imaginative layers of meaning to our gathering places or buildings. What would the Square at Trade and Tryon be without the four sculptures by Raymond Kaskey? They have become distinctive, tangible symbols of our shared history. Because they are public, they are accessible to those who might not go to museums and in that sense serve as a valuable cultural and educational resources. Public art often serves a need identified by an agency, stakeholders and community members engaged in the selection of artists. The general perception of community taste in artwork in Charlotte is traditional and conservative. That perception will expand, as the community is changing and seems to be hungry for innovative work. Through a carefully orchestrated and inclusive process, it is my role on behalf of ASC and the Public Art Commission to offer the community the highest quality of talent in the public art field today. I hope that we are challenging community taste and raising expectations and possibilities.

How does the ASC go about selecting artists and public art? What process do you follow?

ASC uses a community-based process to select artists, and the work is the responsibility of the Public Art Commission, a nine-member board appointed by the City, the County and ASC. Members are drawn from the fields of art and design, education, business and the community at large. Commissioners chair and serve on the artist selection panels, which are comprised of facility or site stakeholders, the architect or engineer for the site and community members. Elected officials may also choose to participate. Once ASC knows the work plan and projects for the coming year, the projects are advertised on our website. We mail a "Call to Artists" to approximately 1,500 artists, advertising new projects and directing them to the ASC website for project descriptions and application information. We also advertise nationally through the Americans for the Arts Public Art Network listserv and through the NC Arts Council listserv.

Numerous selection panels are convened each year to review written and visual submissions by applicants. Panelists decide upon a shortlist of artists for each project and these individuals are invited to Charlotte for interviews. Each panel selects a finalist and alternate which are then referred to the Public Art Commission for review and approval. The Commission's recommendations are sent to the ASC Board of Directors for review and ASC contracts with the artists. The process is labor intensive and the Public Art Commissioners give many hours of service to ensure that the City and County have talented artists creating new projects.

What projects are coming online? Which projects are you particularly excited about?

ASC has seven new projects coming to completion. The Rolfe Neill Tribute sculpture by artist Larry Kirkland is a privately funded artwork sited on the entry plaza of ImaginOn. This project is one of the most important civic gestures for Charlotte since the statues on the Square. Inside ImaginOn, a beautiful pair of bronze sculptures by the team of Jim Hirschfield and Sonya Ishii focus on the theme of storytelling. Just two blocks away, five artists are completing artwork for the Arena. Each one promises to be spectacular, and all focus on the theme of Charlotte's history – past, present and future. Outside there are elegant carved granite benches by Paul Sires and colorful bobbin columns and sculptures surrounding the building by Andrew Leicester setting the tone for the Arena as an entertainment venue. Inside are two monumental photographic ceramic murals by Mike Mandel, a brilliantly colored terrazzo lobby floor by Thomas Sayre and two large-scale oil on canvas murals by Tommie Robinson opposite the escalator banks. We believe this concentration of new works will raise the expectations of what public art can mean for the community. In the coming year, we are moving forward with a major project at the new County Courthouse, the Little Sugar Creek Greenway, Third Ward's West Park and artwork for an eastside sportsplex.

What is the civic value of public art? Why is it worth the expenditure of public tax dollars?

Public art tells the story of who we are as a community and animates our city. It often serves as a catalyst and collaborator in urban design and development efforts, in neighborhoods and in celebrating our diverse identities. Is it worth the tax dollars? Yes, and the expenditure is minimal per citizen. For example, the FY 06 City public art budget funded by tax dollars is $255,500, and the current City population is 651,101. This is a 39 cent investment per citizen this year. Public art is vital to making Charlotte a vibrant, colorful and memorable city that will inspire for generations to come. ⏻

CHARLOTTE VIEWPOINT TEAM

Mark Peres, Editor

A native Californian, Mark grew up in New York and Florida. He is a graduate of Rollins College, where he studied history and philosophy of religion, and The Florida State University College of Law. Since arriving in Charlotte with his wife and daughter, Mark has embraced the city as home. Mark is an entrepreneur and writer. He finds joy in the liberal arts, the creativity of friends, and being involved in a great city.

Carolie Bartol, Production & Design

No matter where she's wandered, Carolie has always known she'd find her way home to North Carolina. After years spent touring the U.S. and Canada with theatre and the circus, co-owning a restaurant, working as a wardrobe mistress in Ireland and teaching outdoor education in the beautiful NC mountains, she settled in Charlotte's Third Ward for three very happy years. She and her husband now live in Sasebo, Japan, though they both hope to return to Charlotte permanently once his tour of duty is over. Carolie enjoys her work as a freelance graphic designer, copywriter and professional storyteller.

Michael Carson, Columnist

Although he was born in Germany and spent most of his childhood years living overseas with his family, Michael has always been a North Carolinian at heart. After graduating from UNC at Chapel Hill, Michael worked for Bank of America and lived in Charlotte's majestic Third Ward. Michael now lives in Chapel Hill with his young son, Casius Michael David. Michael is attending the UNC at Chapel Hill's Law School and Business School in pursuit of his JD and MBA. Some of Michael's favorite Charlotte pastimes included attending the Symphony at the Blumenthal Performing Arts Center, watching plays at Spirit Square, drinking a glass of wine at Cuvée, grabbing a Black & Tan at Ri-Ra Irish Pub, and going to Alexander Michael's for a veggie burger and fries.

Paul Cotter, Photographer

As a contributing photographer for Charlotte ViewPoint, Paul loves to explore the city and capture interesting Uptown perspectives. Paul's an award-winning writer and creative director for Luquire George Andrews advertising agency. He's also been an avid photographer for 25 years. A native of Buffalo, New York, Paul lives in First Ward's Garden District with his wife Bonnie and their two kids, Ben and Jade. When he's not strolling with his Nikon digital camera, he enjoys working out at the Dowd "Y" and walking to Alexander Michael's pub for the occasional Guinness.

Jennifer Garner, Interviewer

Jennifer Garner grew up in Greensboro and came to Charlotte to attend Queens College. After working in higher education across the country, she returned to the Queen City in 2003 to work at her alma mater. Jennifer is enjoying the many changes that happened to Charlotte while she was gone and loves interviewing the interesting people for the Q&A. When not attending alumni events, Jennifer loves to cook, travel internationally and is in two book clubs. A former actress in college, Jennifer would love to hit the boards again in Charlotte.

Angela Lindsay, Columnist

A lawyer by profession, Angela Lindsay discovered her passion for the written word upon writing her first story at nine years old. The Charlotte native relocated back to the Queen City in 2003 from Los Angeles where she was working with the management company of a Grammy-nominated artist. She has returned to the field of law and contributes frequently as a freelance writer for several local and national publications. Currently, she is the associate producer of an award-winning independent film entitled Coffee, Tea or Milk and is active in various other activities and organizations. In her free time, she enjoys watching football, baking desserts and playing billiards.

Dennis Marsoun, Columnist

Dennis has been slowly moving south for the past 25 years, first to Pittsburgh, then to Virginia Beach and finally to Charlotte. Having spent the majority of that time traveling the country while working in the technology industry, Dennis has visited many of the major cities in America. Coupling traveling with a passion for running, he often gets to see sections of a city that most miss. Dennis is actively involved in the Friends of Fourth Ward, a community group located in Uptown Charlotte, and is in charge of membership development. A recent career change has put Dennis in the Real Estate industry. He acts primarily as a Buyers Agent in the Uptown Charlotte marketplace.

Karen Martin, Columnist

Karen Martin arrived in the Queen City in 1994 and has been known to point to certain landmarks and say, "I remember when…." With a Masters Degree in communications from Syracuse University, she sometimes admits to being a former television news reporter, but prefers to talk about the wonderful experiences she has had as a freelance newspaper and magazine writer – a vocation that has allowed her to explore the Charlotte area, its trends and its residents. Karen lived in Dilworth, Myers Park and Elizabeth before settling in Davidson with her husband and twin children. In addition to writing, her passions include real estate and theatre.

Christina Ritchie, Columnist

Davidson College brought this Yankee south. Embracing the liberal arts education, Christina particularly enjoyed painting and performing on stage. After graduating in 2003 with a degree in English and a minor in Spanish, Christina traded in her Jersey tags for North Carolina ones. She currently works as a project manager with MultiLingual Solutions, Inc. While she is reluctantly becoming a type-A workaholic, she still loves theater and visual arts, is an avid reader, and enjoys painting when she can find the time.

Russell Shuler, Photographer

Having directed photographers as an art director for the last quarter century, Russell decided to get behind the camera himself for a change. What he found is that it's a lot more fun than most jobs. Except, of course, when he is producing a stained glass commission for some lucky client. It was 1990, just after Hugo blew through, that Russell joined the ranks of so many Charlotteans not from here, but here now. Fran, his wife of 25 years, is his biggest cheerleader. Then there are the two girls Ashley and Sara Lynn. And, of course, Jenny the golden retriever.

Christa Wagner, Columnist

Christa is one of the few Charlotteans who can claim to have been born and raised in the Queen City. She graduated from Davidson College in 2002 and returned to her hometown to pursue journalism and environmental activism. She now works full time for the Sierra Club, the nation's largest grassroots environmental organization. She has also written for Charlotte Taste *magazine and interned in the planning department of the Town of Davidson.*

Jill Walker, Columnist

Originally from New York, Jill has lived in Charlotte for 24 years, 20 of those in Dilworth. She has been a strong advocate for her neighborhood through the many challenges that growth presents, always striving to find the right balance between preservation and progress. Whether standing up for her neighborhood or standing up for the pledge of allegiance, she always likes to stand for something. Besides her husband, and three children whose lives and schools have occupied much of her time, she is interested in a wide range of subjects, including politics, current events, cooking, writing and, most recently, sailing.

PHOTO CREDITS